W9-BWI-726

TENSIONS IN
MORAL THEOLOGY

Other Books by Charles E. Curran

Toward an American Catholic Moral Theology
Directions in Fundamental Moral Theology
Directions in Catholic Social Ethics
American Catholic Social Ethics: Twentieth-Century Approaches
Moral Theology: A Continuing Journey
Transition and Tradition in Moral Theology
Issues in Sexual and Medical Ethics
Catholic Moral Theology in Dialogue
New Perspectives in Moral Theology

Tensions in
Moral Theology

CHARLES E. CURRAN

UNIVERSITY OF NOTRE DAME PRESS
NOTRE DAME, IN

Library of Congress Cataloging-in-Publication Data

Curran, Charles E.
    Tensions in moral theology.

    Includes index.
    1. Christian ethics — Catholic authors.   2. Sex —
Religious aspects — Catholic Church.   3. Church and
social problems — Catholic Church.   4. Catholic
Church — Doctrines.   I. Title.
BJ1249.C83   1988   241'.042   87-40622
ISBN 0-268-01866-9

Manufactured in the United States of America

To the Church of Rochester

which has nourished, sustained, and challenged me

Contents

Introduction

The tensions existing in Catholic moral theology these days are well known. The most obvious indication of such strains is the action taken by Vatican and other church authorities against a number of Roman Catholic moral theologians. However, the very existence of tensions in moral theology is not something to be deplored. If there were no existing strains, moral theology would no longer be a living discipline both in the church and in the academy. Without doubt the tensions are more strident today than they should be, but moral theology should always experience a number of tensions.

The essays brought together in this volume were written over an eighteen-month period on different subject matters in moral theology. By their very nature no organic unity exists among these separate studies. However, a common thread runs through all the essays to illustrate well the tensions affecting moral theology at the present time.

The primary source of the tensions in moral theology today comes from the changing times in which we live. Moral theology as a part of Roman Catholic theology and as a discipline in the service of the Catholic Church inevitably experiences the changes and strains that have been part and parcel of Roman Catholicism since the Second Vatican Council. At the same time moral theology deals with the numerous questions and issues being raised in a changing society and world. However, it is not merely a question of new and changing issues, for these changes also have an effect on the discipline and methodology of moral theology itself. All the studies in this volume illustrate this fundamental tension facing moral theology today. In addition the individual essays also deal with many of the other contemporary tensions.

The first three chapters directly discuss the justification of theological and practical dissent from noninfallible hierarchical church teaching and thus deal head on with the most serious strains in contemporary moral theology. The church in general and moral theology in particular will always know the tension of creative fidelity to the word and work of Jesus. The church cannot merely repeat what has been said in the past but must make the word and work of Jesus incarnate in the historical and cultural circumstances of our day. The different offices and roles of the hierarchical teaching office and the theological function mean there will always be an inevitable tension between the two. However, the failure of the hierarchical teaching office to recognize the possibility and at times the legitimacy of theological and practical dissent in noninfallible teaching greatly exacerbates this tension today.

The second chapter focuses on the relationship between the church and the academy — a relationship that has known great turbulence over the centuries. Here too the problem of the proper relationship between truth and freedom exists. The question has frequently been asked about the compatibility between Catholic and being a university. This chapter argues for the need for academic freedom for Catholic theology and for Catholic institutions of higher learning. Despite the inevitable tensions academic freedom ultimately serves the best interest of theology in the Roman Catholic Church.

The fourth and fifth chapters deal with sexual morality and sexual ethics. The tensions between authoritative church teaching and much of Catholic theology and practice have centered on sexual questions. As a result of authoritative hierarchical intervention, Catholic theologians have not really been free to devleop a more credible and systematic sexual ethics. However, the existing tensions in Catholic sexual morality and sexual teaching do not spring only from the problem of intervention by church authority. Chapter five compares the methodologies involved in official Catholic social teachings with the methodologies involved in official Catholic sexual teachings. The different approaches at work in the two areas in my judgment only aggravate the tensions experienced in Catholic sexual teaching today.

The methodological approach to Catholic social teaching developed in chapter five introduces the discussion of social ethics found in the next four chapters that deal with economic issues as well as with questions of peace and war. The bishops of the United States have made an outstanding contribution to Catholic social teaching in their two recent pastoral letters on peace and the economy. Chapters six through nine often include analysis and criticism of these two important documents. As pointed out in this book, the moral methodologies supporting these teachings and the "ecclesial methodology" in the drafting of the two pastoral letters of the United States bishops contrast sharply with the corresponding approaches to sexual ethics and sexual teaching. These tensions in contemporary Catholic social ethics well illustrate many of the tensions that will always be present in moral theology.

Perhaps the most significant question in social ethics is the relationship between the community and the individual. Catholic social teaching has employed the concept of the common good in an effort to show that no real opposition should be present between the two. Chapter seven maintains that the common good still remains an important cornerstone of Catholic social ethics, even though the content of the common good has changed in the light of changing circumstances.

The issue of unity and diversity within the church is a perennial question. The United States bishops and their pastoral letters on social issues underscore the different levels of moral discourse. The bishops call for unity on the level of ethical principles and universal Catholic teaching, while recognizing that other Catholics might disagree with the particular judgments they make on specific issues. I basically agree with such an approach to the problem, but more tensions seem to exist than the United States bishops recognize. In their pastoral letter on peace and the nuclear question the West German bishops do not appeal to an independent principle of discrimination and seem to deny the existence of such a universal and independent moral principle, even though the United States bishops strongly insist that this principle must be accepted by all Catholics. The existence of many pastoral letters in various countries on the nuclear question and the differences among them well illustrate the inevitable strains between the particular and the universal in a church which claims the name "catholic."

Christian moral theory and practice always experience the tension between eschatological fullness and the present reality affected not only by the loving work of the creator and redeemer but also by the imperfection, incompleteness, and sinfulness which will always characterize human existence in this world. In this light the United States bishops in their pastoral letter do not call for unilateral nuclear disarmament, even though they do negatively criticize much of the existing nuclear policies of the United States.

Contemporary Catholic social teaching and ethics have also brought to the fore the question of the audience for which such teaching is intended and the tensions between a moral teaching grounded in human reason and experience and a teaching grounded in biblical and faith warrants. Much discussion has been evident in the last two decades within Roman Catholicism about what is unique in Christian ethics. In my judgment no unique, specific content in Christian morality exists which is not in principle also open to acceptance by non-Christians. This question lies just below the surface in these chapters.

Contemporary Catholic ethics continues to explore the way in which judgments of conscience are formed. An older approach definitely insisted on a deductive model by which principles were applied to particular cases. However, more recently emphasis has been put on judgments made through a subjective connaturality in a more inductive manner. The documents proposing official Catholic social teaching show this same development. Within the two pastoral letters of the United States bishops such connatural judgments seemed to exercise a more prominent place than the bishops themselves were willing to acknowledge explicitly. Chapter nine attempts to throw some light on this contemporary tension.

The last chapter raises the question of being both Catholic and American. The history and self-understanding of Roman

Catholicism in the United States can best be understood in the light of this problematic — Can the church be both Catholic and American at one and the same time? This tension will always be present because at times the church will learn from the culture but at other times it must strongly condemn and criticize the culture. Such a tension derives from the relationship between the church and the world and between the church universal and the church particular. It is important to recall that the tension is not only between the church in the United States and the church universal, but similar tensions exist between all the local churches and the church universal. Unfortunately, such tensions in the Roman Catholic Church between the universal church and the local church are aggravated at the present time because since Vatican II no significant structural change has been brought about to give more attention to the role of the college of bishops and of the local churches.

Thus the studies gathered together in this volume well illustrate the tensions existing in Catholic moral theology today. An attempt has been made throughout to point out that some of these tensions will always be present, but other strains are more pointed today than they should be.

I have written this volume in the midst of the strains I feel in doing Catholic moral theology today. However, I have been consoled and strengthened by the support and solidarity of so many colleagues, students, friends, and acquaintances. Words are insufficient to express my gratitude for such support and solidarity. In addition I am particularly grateful to all those who assisted me in the writing of this book. Above all I am grateful to Donnalee Dox Kulhawy for typing the manuscript for this book and also for the many other letters and manuscripts she has done for me. Her dedication, efficiency, and cheerfulness have taken away many of the tensions often associated with preparing a manuscript for publication. David Power, the chair of the Department of Theology at The Catholic University of America, and Johann Klodzen, the administrative assistant of that department, have been most supportive in general and in facilitating my writing. Again I want to acknowledge publicly the help of the library staff at the Mullen Library of The Catholic University of America — Bruce Miller, David Gilson, and Mary Liu, as well as Carolyn Lee. John Ehmann of the University of Notre Dame Press continues to assist me with his editorial help and advice. Julia Fleming prepared the index.

I gratefully acknowledge the permission of the following publishers and periodicals to republish materials which first appeared in their publications: The College Theology Society, for "My Theological Dissent: The Issues," which first appeared in the 1986 proceedings of their convention; *The Journal of the American Academy of Religion*, for "Academic Freedom, Theology, and Catholic Institutions of Higher Learning"; *America* and *The National Catholic Reporter*, which first published different parts of "Personal Reaction and Response"; *The Christian Century*, for "The Development of Sexual Ethics in Contemporary Roman Catholicism"; *Theology Today*, for "Official Catholic Social and Sexual Teachings: A Methodological Comparison"; The State University College of Arts and Science at Geneseo, for "Ethical Principles of Catholic Social Teaching in the United States Bishops' Letter on the Economy," which first appeared in the *Proceedings of the Eighteenth Conference on Value Inquiry*; The University Press of America, for "Official Catholic Social Teaching and the Common Good," which appeared in Oliver F. Williams and John W. Houck, eds., *The Common Good and U.S. Capitalism*; The Festschrift in honor of Sean O'Riordan, for "Official Catholic Social Teaching and Conscience"; *Horizons*, for "Being Catholic and Being American."

1: My Theological Dissent: The Issues

On August 18, 1986, I was handed a letter dated July 25, 1986, from Cardinal Joseph Ratzinger, the prefect of the Vatican Congregation for the Doctrine of the Faith, informing me that one who dissents from the magisterium as I do is not suitable nor eligible to teach Catholic theology.[1] At the same time Archbishop James A. Hickey, archbishop of Washington and chancellor of The Catholic University of America, informed me that he was initiating the process to withdraw my canonical mission to teach in the ecclesiastical faculty of theology at the university.

The action taken by the Vatican was not a surprise. I had been informed in August 1979 that I was under investigation by the Congregation for the Doctrine of the Faith. The letter from the congregation was signed by Cardinal Franjo Seper, the then prefect of the congregation, and included sixteen pages of "Observations" to which I was asked to reply. This letter initiated a process and a correspondence between the congregation and myself which lasted until the summer of 1986. As the process continued the signs became more ominous. In a May 10, 1983, letter Cardinal Ratzinger asked me to indicate in writing whether or not I wanted to revise my positions in clear public dissent from the magisterium. In an accompanying set of "Observations" these issues were listed as: artificial contraception, indissolubility of marriage, abortion, euthanasia, masturbation, premarital intercourse, homosexual acts, direct sterilization, and artificial insemination. My response once again explained my nuanced positions on these questions and defended the right of Catholic theologians to dissent from noninfallible hierarchial teaching. However, in my judgment the handwriting was on the wall.

I received a September 17, 1985, letter from Cardinal Ratzinger concluding the inquiry. I was asked to reconsider and retract those positions which violate the conditions necessary for a professor to be called a Catholic theologian. This letter was handed to me by Archbishop Hickey, the chancellor of The Catholic University of America, and by Cardinal Joseph Bernardin, the chair of the Board of Trustees of the university. After that initial meeting we met three other times in an attempt to work out a compromise. In conscience I could not retract my positions, but I proposed some possible compromises. With the same intention I asked for an informal meeting with the officials of the Congregation for the Doctrine of the Faith, which took place at the Vatican on March 8. After that meeting a joint statement was released to the press.

After the meeting at the Vatican I received strong support from theological colleagues throughout the world, from my dean and the majority of my colleagues at Catholic University, from my students, and from many Catholics. However, I guarded against raising my hopes that the matter could be resolved through some acceptable compromise. Thus, I was not surprised in the summer of 1986 when I received the letter informing me that I was no longer suitable nor eligible to exercise the function of a professor of Catholic theology.

This chapter will deal with the theological issues raised by this dispute, whereas chapter two will consider the academic issues involved in the controversy. The third chapter will discuss my personal reactions and responses to the actions taken against me. Before discussing the particular issues involved in this case, it is important to recognize the context and the presuppositions for the discussion.

Context and Presuppositions

The general context for this chapter and for the entire case is that of the Roman Catholic Church and Catholic theology.

I have made it very clear that I am a believing Catholic and intend to do Catholic theology. Despite my intentions I still might be wrong, but I maintain that my positions are totally acceptable for a Catholic theologian and believing Roman Catholic.

The mission of the entire church is to be faithful to the word and work of Jesus. God's revelation has been handed over and entrusted to the church, which faithfully hands this down from generation to generation through the assistance of the Holy Spirit. Roman Catholicism recognizes that revelation was closed at the end of apostolic times, but revelation itself develops and is understood in the light of the different historical and cultural circumstances of the hearers and doers of the word.

Roman Catholic faith and theology have strongly disagreed with the emphasis on the scripture alone, for the scripture must always be understood in light of the thought patterns of our own time. The Catholic insistence on the scripture and tradition recognized the need to develop and understand God's revelation in Jesus Christ in the light of the contemporary circumstances. The early councils of the fourth, fifth, and subsequent centuries illustrate how in matters touching the very heart of faith — the understanding of God and of Jesus Christ — the living church felt the need to go beyond the words of the scripture, to understand better and more adequately the revelation of God. Thus, the Christian Church taught there are three persons in God and two natures in Jesus. Fidelity to the traditon does not mean merely repeating the very words of the scripture or of older church teaching. The Christian tradition is a living tradition, and fidelity involves a creative fidelity which seeks to preserve in its own time and place the incarnational principle. Creative fidelity is the task of the church in bearing witness to the word and work of Jesus.

In carrying out its call to creative fidelity to the word and work of Jesus the church is helped by the papal and episcopal roles in the church. The existence of this pastoral teaching function of pope and bishops in the church must be recognized by all. However, much development has occurred in the understanding of the exact nature of that teaching office, how it is exercised, and what is its relationship to the other functions connected with the offices of pope and bishops in the church. Much of the following discussion will center on what is often called today the ordinary magisterium of the papal office. This term "ordinary magisterium" understood in this present sense has only been in use since the nineteenth century.[2] A Catholic must recognize the pastoral office of teaching given to pope and bishops but also should realize that this teaching function has been exercised in different ways over the years.[3]

These aspects briefly mentioned in this opening section are very important and could be developed at much greater length and depth. However, in this chapter they are being recalled as the necessary context and presuppositions for the discussion of the issues raised by the case involving the Congregation for the Doctrine of the Faith and myself. I understand myself to be a Catholic theologian and a Catholic believer, who recognizes the call of the church to be faithful in a creative way to the word and work of Jesus and who gratefully and loyally accepts the papal and episcopal functions in the church.

This chapter will now focus on what in my judgment are the primary issues involved in my case. In the process I will state briefly my own position on these issues. Four issues will be considered: the role of the theologian, the possibility of public theological dissent from some noninfallible teachings, the possibility and right of dissent by the Christian faithful, and the justice and fairness of the process. The September 17, 1985, letter from Cardinal Ratzinger calls upon me to retract my positions in the following specific areas: contraception and sterilization; abortion and euthanasia; masturbation, premarital intercourse, and homosexual acts; the indissolubility of marriage. However, as Richard McCormick perceptively points out, these particular moral questions and agreement or disagreement with my positions on these questions do not constitute the major points of contention in the dispute between the congregation and myself.[4] These are important topics, but they are primarily illustrative of the more fundamental issues involved. I have developed and defended my positions on these moral questions in my responses to the congregation and in many other writings.

The Role of the Theologian

Much has been written on the role of the theologian and the relationship between the function of bishops and theologians in the church. Since it is impossible to add to this discussion in this short space, the purpose here is to raise up the underlying issues involved in the present controversy. Many and probably the majority of Catholic theologians writing today see the role of the Catholic theologian as somewhat independent and cooperative in relationship to the hierarchical office and not delegated or derivative from the role of pope and bishops. The theologian is a scholar who studies critically, thematically, and systematically Christian faith and action. Such a scholar must theologize within the Catholic faith context and must give due importance to all the *loci theologici*, including the teaching of the hierarchical magisterium. The Catholic theologian to be such must give the required assent to official church teaching, but the theologian does not derive his or her theological office from delegation by the hierarchical officeholders. The pastoral teaching function of pope and bishops is connected with their offices in the church and differs from the teaching role of theologians. Note that I have described this understanding of the Catholic theologian as somewhat independent and cooperative with regard to the hierarchical role in the church. That independence is modified by the call of the theologian and all believers to give due assent to the pastoral teaching role of bishops and pope.

However, a very different understanding of the role of the theologian is found in more recent church legislation. The new Code of Canon Law, which came into effect in the fall of 1983, and the apostolic constitution for ecclesiastical faculties and universities, *Sapientia Christiana*, understand the role of the theologian as primarily derived from the hierarchical teaching office and functioning by reason of delegation given by the hierarchical teaching office. A good illustration of this understanding of the theologian as delegate and representative of the hierarchical teaching office is found in canon 812 of the new Code of Canon Law: "Those who teach theological subjects in any institute of higher studies must have a mandate from the competent ecclesiastical authority." According to the code this mandate is required for all those who teach theology in any Catholic institution of higher learning. Earlier versions of the code spoke of a "canonical mission" instead of a mandate. *Sapientia Christiana*, the apostolic constitution governing ecclesiastical faculties, requires a canonical mission from the chancellor for those teaching disciplines concerning faith or morals.[5] The final version of the code uses the word mandate and not canonical mission because canonical mission appears to imply the assignment of a person to an ecclesiastical office.[6] The implication of this new canon and of other recent legislation is that the Catholic theologian in a Catholic institution officially exercises the function of teaching in that school through a delegation from the bishop. The role of the Catholic theologian is thus derived from the hierarchical teaching function and juridically depends upon it.

It seems there has been an interesting, even contradictory, development in Catholic documents within the past few years. The more theoretical documents seem to recognize a somewhat independent and cooperative role for theologians, whereas the legislative documents understand the theological role as derivative and delegated from the hierarchical teaching office. Without doubt, from the nineteenth century until recent times the role of the theologian was seen as subordinate to and derivative from the hierarchical teaching office. However, Vatican Council II in its general ecclesiology and in its understanding of theologians can be interpreted to adopt a more cooperative and somewhat independent understanding of the role of theologians vis-à-vis the hierarchical magisterium.[7] The cooperative model does not deny the official role of the hierarchical office in protecting and proclaiming the faith, but theology is a scholarly discipline distinct from but related to the proclamation of the faith by the hierarchical teaching office. However, canonists recognize that recent canonical legislation including the new Code of Canon Law understands the theological function as derivative from the hierarchical teaching function. In the older Code of Canon Law there was no requirement for theologians in Catholic institutions to have a canonical mandate or mission to teach theology. The older code saw the role of the ordinary, or diocesan bishop, in terms of negative vigilance with regard to individual teachers of theology and not one of positive deputation.[8]

Doubtless present church legislation tends to see the theological function as derivative from the hierarchical teaching function. However, very many Catholic theologians today appeal to more recent developments in Catholic understanding to substantiate a somewhat cooperative and independent understanding of the theological role vis-à-vis the hierarchical role. The correspondence between the Congregation for the Doctrine of the Faith and myself never explicitly goes into this question as such, but the congregation is operating out of a derivative understanding of the role of the theologian, while I adopt the somewhat independent and cooperative understanding.

In my understanding the teaching function is committed to the whole church. In addition, a special pastoral teaching office is given to pope and bishops in the church. As important as this hierarchical teaching function is, it is not identical with the total teaching function of the entire church. Many teaching roles exist in the church. The teaching role of theologians does not depend on an office in the church but finds its authority in the faithful expertise of the scholar. This understanding of teaching authority in the Catholic Church, which is proposed by many contemporary Catholic theologians, has been called a pluralistic approach as distinguished from the hierocratic approach which reduces the teaching authority in the church to the teaching offices of pope and bishops.[9]

Public Theological Dissent from Some Noninfallible Hierarchical Church Teachings

The correspondence from the congregation indicates that the problem is public dissent from some hierarchical noninfallible teaching, not merely private dissent. However, the meaning of "public" is never developed. The entire investigation centers on my theological writings, so the only logical conclusion is that public here refers to theological writings. Private dissent apparently means something that is not written and is not spoken publicly.

From the very beginning the position of the congregation surprised me because the congregation was denying the legitimate possibility of public theological dissent from the noninfallible teachings under discussion. My surprise was rooted in the fact that some Catholic bishops and very many theologians have recognized the possibility of such public theological dissent.

In 1979, after receiving the first set of "Observations" from the congregation, I had the feeling that the investigation would soon focus clearly on the manner and mode of public dissent. Past experience was the basis for this judgment. Recall that in 1968 I acted as the spokesperson for a group ultimately numbering over 600 theologians and issued a public statement at a press conference which concluded that Catholic spouses may responsibly decide according to their conscience that artificial contraception in some circumstances is permissible and even necessary to preserve and foster the values and sacredness of marriage. In response to this statement the trustees of The Catholic University of America on September 5, 1969, mandated an inquiry in accord with academic due process to determine if the Catholic University professors involved in this dissent had violated by their declarations and actions their responsibilities to the university.[10]

A few months later the object of the inquiry had definitely changed. "Hence the focus of the present inquiry is on the style and method whereby some faculty members expressed personal dissent from papal teaching, and apparently helped organize additional public dissent to such teaching."[11] The Board of Trustees did not question the right of a scholar to dissent from noninfallible church teaching. In the context of the inquiry it became clear that public and organized dissent referred primarily to holding a press conference and to actively soliciting other theologians to sign the original statement. The primary question of public dissent thus was not regular theological publication but the use of the more popular media. In response to this new focus the professors subject to the inquiry at Catholic University through their counsel pointed out the changed focus but went on to show that such public and organized dissent in the popular media was a responsible action by Catholic theologians. The shift in the focus of the inquiry seemed to come from the fact that the trustees, including the bishops on the Board of Trustees, were willing to recognize the possibility of even public dissent in theological journals as being legitimate but objected to the use of the popular media. The faculty inquiry committee fully agreed with the thrust of the argument proposed by the professors, and the professors were exonerated in this hearing.

However, to my surprise the correspondence from the congregation never moved explicitly in the direction of the manner and mode of dissent and even at times the use of popular media. The conclusion logically follows from the position taken by the congregation that the only acceptable form of dissent on these issues is that which is neither written nor spoken publicly.

The controversy explicitly deals with dissent on the specific questions under dispute. However, the correspondence seems to imply that the theologian cannot legitimately dissent from any noninfallible hierarchical teaching. I have always pointed out in the correspondence that I have been dealing with the noninfallible hierarchical teaching office. This position was explicitly accepted by the congregation in all of the correspondence prior to the September 17, 1985, letter to me from Cardinal Ratzinger. A very few Catholic theologians have maintained that the teaching on artificial contraception is infallible from the ordinary teaching of pope and bishops throughout the world.[12] However, this position is not held by the vast majority of theologians and has not been proposed or defended by the congregation. One could also maintain that the Catholic teaching on divorce is infallible by reason of the teaching of the Council of Trent. However, the phrasing of the canons with regard to the indissolubility of marriage, the attempt not to condemn the practice of *"oiconomia"* of the Greek Church, and the somewhat broad understanding of *"anathema sit"* at that time of Trent argue against the infallible nature of the Catholic Church's teaching on the indissolubility of marriage. Accepted standard textbooks, such as that of Pierre Adnès, recognize that the teaching on absolute intrinsic indissolubility is not infallible.[13] Thus, my position all along has been that I have never denied an infallible teaching of the church.

However, in the September 17 letter Cardinal Ratzinger seems to claim that the assent of faith is somehow involved in my case. I have strenuously maintained that the assent of faith is not involved. We are dealing with the *obsequium religiosum* (the exact meaning of this term will be discussed later) which is due in cases of noninfallible teaching. I have never been explicitly accused of denying an infallible teaching. However, it is very clear that the congregation definitely maintains that the *obsequium religiosum* due to noninfallible teaching does not allow the theologian to dissent publicly in these cases.

Cardinal Ratzinger himself has called the distinction between infallible and noninfallible teaching "legalistic." Only in this century have theologians made this distinction in such a sharp way. "When one affirms that noninfallible doctrines, even though they make up part of the teaching of the church, can be legitimately contested, one ends up by destroying the practice of the Christian life and reduces the faith to a collection of doctrines." Abortion, divorce, and homosexuality, even with a thousand distinctions that can be made, are acts that go against Christian faith.[14] Ratzinger deemphasizes the distinction between infallible and noninfallible teaching to help support his position that a theologian cannot dissent publicly from these noninfallible church teachings. What is to be said about Ratzinger's understanding?

Truly the sharp distinction between infallible and noninfallible teaching is recent, for it became prevalent only at the time of the first Vatican Council (1870), which defined the infallibility of the pope. After that time theologians quite rightly distinguished the two levels of teaching and the two different assents which are due to such teachings. All the faithful owe the assent of faith to infallible teaching and the *obsequium religiosum* of intellect and will to authoritative or authentic, noninfallible teaching. The distinction became well entrenched in the theology manuals of the twentieth century before Vatican II.[15] Such a distinction helped to explain that official teaching on some issues had been wrong and had subsequently been corrected (e.g., the condemnation of interest-taking, the need for the intention of procreation to justify conjugal relations). At the time of Vatican Council I and later it was also pointed out that Popes Liberius (+ 366), Vigilius (+ 555), and Honorius (+ 638) all proposed erroneous teachings which were subsequently rejected through theological dissent. Vatican Council II changed many earlier teachings such as those on religious freedom and the relationship of the Roman Catholic Church to other Christian churches and to the true church of Jesus Christ. Scripture scholars for the last generation or so have publicly disagreed with the teachings that were proposed by the Biblical Commission in the first two decades of this century. The theologians thus recognized the distinction between infallible and noninfallible teaching and used it among other purposes to explain why certain earlier errors in church teaching did not refute the Vatican I teaching on papal infallibility. These theologians likewise recognized the possibility of dissent from such noninfallible teaching at times but did not explicitly justify public dissent.[16]

The theologians are not the only ones to use this distinction. *Lumen Gentium*, the Constitution on the Church of the Second Vatican Council, recognizes this distinction between infallible and noninfallible teaching and the two different types of assent which are due (par. 25). The new Code of Canon Law clearly distinguishes between the assent of faith and the *obsequium religiosum* of intellect and will which is due to the authoritative teaching of the pope and college of bishops even when they do not intend to proclaim that doctrine by a definitive act (canon 752). This distinction is thus accepted not only by theologians but also by official documents and by the new Code of Canon Law.

Some theological manuals and many contemporary theologians understand the *obsequium religiosum* owed to authoritative, noninfallible teaching to justify at times the possibility of theological dissent, and at the present time even public dissent. Some bishops' conferences explicitly recognized the legitimacy of dissent from the papal encyclical *Humanae Vitae* issued in 1968. Also documents from bishops' conferences have acknowledged the possibility of public theological dissent from some noninfallible church teaching. The United States bishops in their 1968 pastoral letter "Human Life in Our Day" recognize that in noninfallible teaching a presumption in favor of the magisterium is always present. However, the pastoral letter also acknowledges the legitimacy of public theological dissent from such teaching if the reasons are serious and well-founded, if the manner of the dissent does not question or impugn the teaching authority of the church, and if the dissent is such as not to give scandal.[17] Since I have developed at great length in my correspondence with the congregation both the arguments justifying the possibility of public dissent and the many theologians and others in the church who recognize such a possibility, there is no need to repeat this here.

One significant aspect of the question deserves mention here because of some recent developments — the understanding and translation of *obsequium religiosum*. *Obsequium* has often been translated as submission or obedience. Bishop Christopher Butler was, to my knowledge, the first to translate the word *"obsequium"* as due respect.[18] Francis Sullivan, a Jesuit professor and former dean at the Pontifical Gregorian University in Rome, in his book on the magisterium rejects the translation as "due respect" but still allows the possibility of legitimate, public theological dissent from noninfallible church teaching.[19] (Sullivan strongly defends the distinction between infallible and noninfallible church teaching.[20] He sees the position taken by the Vatican congregation in its correspondence with me as threatening the critical function of the theologian with regard to the nondefinitive teaching of the magisterium. "The idea that Catholic theologians, at any level of education, can only teach the official church position, and present only those positions in their writings, is new and disturbing." Sullivan, who considers his approach "rather moderate" and "standard," has been teaching the possibility of public theological dissent from some noninfallible teaching at the Pontifical Gregorian

University in Rome. Sullivan adds that "no one has ever questioned what I teach.") Sullivan claims that "submission" and not "due respect" is the proper translation of *obsequium*, but the Gregorian University professor still recognizes the possibility and legitimacy of public theological dissent from authoritative, noninfallible teaching.

The English text of the Code of Canon Law found in the commentary commissioned by the Canon Law Society of America and authorized by the executive committee of the National Conference of Catholic Bishops in the United States translates *obsequium* as respect.[21] Ladislas Orsy in a recent commentary on canon 752 recognizes difficulties in translating *obsequium* but opts for respect. Orsy also accepts the possibility of legitimate public dissent from some authoritative, noninfallible teaching.[22] The discussion over the proper understanding and translation of *obsequium* has been an occasion for many to recognize the possibility of legitimate public dissent from some noninfallible church teaching.

Without doubt church documents, the Code of Canon Law, theologians in general, and canonists in general have accepted the importance of the distinction between infallible and noninfallible hierarchical teaching. Although I believe the distinction between infallible and noninfallible teaching is very important and necessary, there is a need to say more in dealing with the possibility of public dissent. I disagree with Cardinal Ratzinger's attempt to smooth over somewhat the clear distinction between infallible and noninfallible teaching, but his remarks show the need to say something in addition to the distinction between infallible and noninfallible teaching. What about the danger of reducing the Christian faith in practice to a small, abstract core? Are abortion, divorce, and homosexuality, even with nuanced distinctions, acts which go against Christian faith?

In my own comments about this case in the popular media I have been careful not only to use the distinction between infallible and noninfallible teaching but also to talk about what is core and central to the faith as distinguished from those things that are more removed and peripheral. Also I have consistently spoken about the right to dissent publicly from *some* noninfallible church teaching. The distinction between infallible and noninfallible church teaching is absolutely necessary but not sufficient. The older theology tried to deal with questions of the relationship of church teaching to the core of faith through the use of "theological notes." These notes and their opposites in terms of censures recognized the complexity by categorizing many different types of noninfallible teaching.[23] In a true sense a need exists today to redevelop the concept of theological notes in the light of the realities of the present time.

As important as the concept of infallible teaching is, some very significant limitations are involved in it. Infallible teaching, especially of the extraordinary type by pope or council, has usually come in response to an attack on or a denial of something central to the faith. However, some points which have never been denied by believers, such as the existence of God, have never been defined by the extraordinary hierarchical teaching office. Something can be infallible by reason of the ordinary teachings of the pope and all the bishops, but the conditions required for such infallibility are often difficult to verify. On the other hand, the limits and imperfections of any infallible teaching have been rightly recognized. Infallible teaching itself is always open to development, better understanding, and even purification. Thus, one must be careful when speaking about infallible teaching both because some things might pertain to the core of faith which have at least not been infallibly taught by the extraordinary teaching function of the pope and bishops and because even infallible teaching itself is open to development and further interpretation. However, in the present discussion the distinction between infallible and noninfallible is very important. It allows me to deal with a limited area—the area of noninfallible teaching.

Within this large area of what is noninfallible it is necessary to recognize various degrees and levels of relationship to faith. Here an updating of the older theological notes would be very useful. True, I have not attempted to develop all the distinctions involved in noninfallible teaching, but in the light of the purposes of the present discussion I have always tried to show that the particular issues under discussion are remote from the central realities of Christian faith.

The Catholic tradition in moral theology has insisted that its moral teaching is based primarily on natural law and not primarily on faith or the scripture. The natural law is understood to be human reason reflecting on human nature. Even those teachings which have some basis in scripture (e.g., the indissolubility of marriage, homosexuality) were also said to be based on natural law. This insistence on the rational nature of Catholic moral teaching recognizes such teaching can and should be shared by all human beings of all faiths and of no faith. Such teachings are thus somewhat removed from the core of Catholic faith as such. The distance of these teachings from the core of faith and the central realities of faith grounds the possibility of legitimate dissent.

In addition, the issues under discussion are specific, concrete, universal moral norms existing in the midst of complex reality. Logic demands that the more specific and complex the reality, the less is the possibility of certitude. Moral norms in my judgment are not the primary, or the only, or the most important concern of moral teaching and of moral theology. Moral teaching deals with general perspectives, values, attitudes, and dispositions as well as norms. Values, attitudes, and dispositions are much more important and far reaching for the moral life than are specific norms. These values and dispositions by their very nature are somewhat more general and can be more universally accepted as necessary for Christian and human life. Within the church all can and should agree that the disciples of Jesus are called to be loving, faithful, hopeful, caring people who strive to live out the reality of the paschal mystery. Disrespect for persons, cheating, slavery, dishonesty, and injustice are always wrong. However, the universal binding force of specific, concrete material norms cannot enjoy the same degree or level of certitude. Norms exist to protect and promote values, but in practice conflicts often arise in the midst of the complexity and specificity involved. Thus the issues under consideration in this case are quite far removed from the core of faith and exist at such a level of complexity and specificity that one has to recognize some possibility of dissent. It is also important to recognize the necessary distinction between the possibility of dissent and the legitimacy of dissent on particular questions. Reasons must be given which are convincing in order to justify the dissent in practice. The central issue involved in the controversy between the Congregation for the Doctrine of the Faith and myself is the possibility of public theological dissent from some noninfallible teaching which is quite remote from the core of faith, heavily dependent on support from human reason, and involved in such complexity and specificity that logically one cannot claim absolute certitude.

A further question has not received much discussion from the Catholic theological community but should at least be raised. We have generally talked about the responsibilities and rights of Catholic theologians in general. Are there any distinctions that must be made concerning theologians? Are the rights and responsibilities of Catholic theologians and the particular right to dissent in these areas the same for all Catholic theologians? Is there a difference between the theologian as teacher and as researcher and writer? Is there a difference if the theologian teaches in a seminary, a college, or a university? In the particular cases under discussion I would develop the thesis that these differences do not affect the possibility and legitimacy of public theological dissent. All of us can agree on the need to explore this question in much greater depth. In addition more attention must be given to the limits of legitimate dissent.

The Christian Faithful and Dissent

A third aspect or issue has not received the attention it needs—the possibility and legitimacy of dissent on the part of the members of the church. In a very true sense my present controversy involves more than merely the role of theologians in the church.

Without doubt much of the friction between theologians and the hierarchical magisterium has occurred on more practical questions, including moral issues touching on sexuality.

The issues are not simply abstract questions about which people speculate, but they involve concrete decisions about specific actions which are to be done. Problems arise in these areas precisely because they involve more than speculation. Here the positions proposed by theologians might have some practical bearing on how people live. All must recognize that the distinction between the roles of bishops and theologians would be much clearer if the role of theologians were restricted to the realm of speculation with no effect on what people do in practice. However, life is not so easily compartmentalized.

Elsewhere I have defended the thesis that on some issues a loyal Catholic may disagree in theory and in practice with the church's noninfallible teaching and still consider oneself a loyal and good Roman Catholic.[24] In a sense, under certain conditions one can speak of a right of the Catholic faithful to dissent from certain noninfallible teachings. In the aftermath of *Humanae Vitae* in 1968 some bishops' conferences recognized that dissent in practice from the encyclical's teaching condemning artificial contraception could be legitimate and did not cut one off from the body of the faithful. The congregation in its correspondence with me has not gone explicitly into this issue. Those who deny the legitimacy of such dissent in practice would seem to face a difficult ecclesiological problem when confronted with the fact that the vast majority of fertile Catholic spouses use artificial contraception. What is the relationship of these spouses to the Roman Catholic Church?

The possibility of legitimate dissent by the faithful stands on its own and is not directly dependent on theological dissent. In my own theologizing I realize how much I have learned from the experience of Christian people. However, the importance of recognizing this possibility and even right on the part of the faithful greatly affects how the theologian functions. If there is such a possibility of dissent, then the individual members of the Catholic Church have a right to know about it. I hasten to add that the individual members also have a right to know what is the official teaching of the church and should be conscious of the dangers of finitude and sin that can skew any human decision. Public dissent by a

Catholic theologian would then be called for not only because theologians must discuss with one another in the attempt to understand better God's word and to arrive at truth but also because the people of God need this information to make their own moral decisions. Thus, for example, in the light of the situation present at the time of the issuance of the encyclical *Humanae Vitae* in 1968 it was important for Roman Catholic spouses to know that they did not have to make a choice between using artificial contraception under some conditions and ceasing to be members of the Roman Catholic Church. The Catholic theologian among others had an obligation to tell this to Catholic spouses.

The possibility for legitimate dissent in practice by the faithful also affects the matter of scandal. The United States bishops in their 1968 letter proposed three conditions under which public theological dissent is in order. One of these conditions is that the dissent be such as not to give scandal. In my correspondence with the congregation I repeatedly asked them for criteria which should govern public theological dissent in the church. No developed criteria were ever forthcoming. However, the April 1983 "Observations" from the congregation mentioned briefly that to dissent publicly and to encourage dissent in others runs the risk of causing scandal.[25]

Scandal in the strict sense is an action or omission which provides another the occasion of sinning. In the broad sense scandal is the wonderment and confusion which are caused by a certain action or omission. The existence of sin and of scandal understood in the strict sense is logically dependent on whether the dissent itself is legitimate.[26] What about scandal as the wonderment and confusion caused among the faithful by public theological dissent? Without doubt in the past a strong tendency existed on the part of the hierarchical leaders of the church to look upon the faithful as poor and ignorant sheep who had to be protected and helped. This same vision and understanding of the ordinary common people also lay behind an older Catholic justification of monarchy and government from above. Catholic social teaching itself has changed in the twentieth century and accepted the need for and importance of democratic political institutions. No longer are the citizens the poor sheep or the "ignorant multitude," to use the phrase employed by Pope Leo XIII. So, too, the members of the church can no longer be considered as poor sheep. Greater importance must be given to their increased education and rights in all areas, including religion.[27]

Perhaps at times theologians, who often associate with people who are well educated, will fail to give enough importance to the danger of disturbing some of the faithful with their teachings. However, in this day and age it seems many more Catholic lay people would be scandalized if theologians were forbidden to discuss publicly important topics of the day such as contraception, divorce, abortion, and homosexuality. These issues are being discussed at great length in all places today, and theologians must be able to enter into the discussion even to the point of dissenting from some official Catholic teaching. In addition, if the faithful can at times dissent in practice and remain loyal Roman Catholics, then they have the right to know what theologians are discussing.

This entire discussion would ultimately be erroneous to confine the question only to the possibility and right of theologians to dissent publicly from some noninfallible teachings. Need for further development and nuancing exists, but on all the moral issues under consideration I have carefully tried to indicate in my writings what in practice are the legitimate possibilities for the faithful. The right of the faithful in this matter definitely colors one's approach to public theological dissent and to the dangers of scandal brought about by such dissent or the lack of it.

Justice and Fairness of the Process

Catholic theology has always emphasized the incarnational principle with its emphasis on visible human structures. Catholic ecclesiology well illustrates this approach by insisting on the church as a visible human community — the people of God with a hierarchical structure. The visible church strives to be a sacrament or sign of the presence of God in the world in and through this visible community. Within the community tensions are bound to be present involving the role of bishops and the role of theologians. Both strive to work for the good of the church, but there will always be tensions. To claim no tension exists would be illusory and ultimately would deny that the church is a living, pilgrim community. The church is always striving to know and live better the word and work of Jesus in the particular historical and cultural circumstances of time and place. The role of the theologian by definition will often be that of probing, exploring, and tentatively pushing the boundaries forward. The hierarchical teaching office must promote such creative and faithful theological activity, while at the same time it must rightly wait until these newer developments emerge more clearly. The church in justice must find ways to deal with this tension in the relationship between theologians and the hierarchical teaching office. The good of the church, the credibility of its teaching office, and the need to protect the rights of all concerned call for just ways of dealing with these inevitable tensions.

The present case raises questions of justice and of the credibility of the teaching office in the church. All recognize that many Catholic theologians publicly dissent from some noninfallible teachings. Likewise many Catholic theologians hold similar positions and some even more radical positions on the moral issues involved in the present case. However, the issues of justice and credibility go much deeper.

First, the congregation must state its position on public theological dissent from noninfallible teaching. Is such dissent ever allowed? If so, under what conditions or criteria? From my correspondence the congregation seems to claim that all public theological dissent is wrong, or at least public dissent on these particular issues is wrong. Does the congregation truly hold such a position? As mentioned earlier, the United States bishops in 1968 in the light of the controversy engendered by *Humanae Vitae* proposed three conditions for justifying public dissent from noninfallible teaching. I have consistently maintained that my dissent has been in accord with these norms. The congregation was unwilling to accept these norms. Does the congregation disagree with the United States bishops and with the vast majority of Catholic theologians?

Archbishop John Quinn, then of Oklahoma City, at the Synod of Bishops in 1974 pointed out the real need to arrive at some consensus and understanding about dissent and urged discussions between representatives of the Holy See and representatives of theologians to arrive at acceptable guidelines governing theological dissent in the church.[28] Archbishop Quinn brought up the same problem again at the Synod of Bishops in 1980.[29] For the good of the church a "real need" to arrive at some guidelines in this area continues.

In addition a need exists for juridical structures which better safeguard justice and the rights of all concerned. Some of the problems with the present procedures of the congregation have already been pointed out in the correspondence. The congregation in a letter to me has defended its procedures because the *"Ratio Agendi"* is not a trial but rather a procedure designed to generate a careful and accurate examination of the contents of published writings by the author. However, since the process can result in severe punishment for the person involved, it seems that such a process should incorporate the contemporary standards of justice found in other juridical proceedings.

One set of problems stems from the fact that the congregation is the prosecutor, the judge, and jury. Some people have objected strongly to the fact that the cardinal prefect has commented publicly on the present case and disagreed in the public media with my position while the case has been in progress. Problems have also been raised against the existing procedures from the viewpoints of the secrecy of the first part of the process, the failure to allow the one being investigated to have counsel, the failure to disclose the accusers and the total record to the accused, and the lack of any substantive appeal process.[30] Many suggestions have been made for improvements in the procedures. The German bishops, for example, have adopted procedures for use in Germany.[31] Cardinal Ratzinger in 1984 admitted that the plenary session of the congregation had decided to revise the current procedures of the congregation. The proposals made by the German Conference of Bishops have been accepted in principle. However, because of the workload and time constraints the decree has not been put into effect.[32]

In 1980 a joint committee of the Catholic Theological Society of America and the Canon Law Society of America was formed to address the question of cooperation between theologians and the hierarchical magisterium in the United States with a view toward developing norms that could be used in settling disputes. The committee prepared a detailed set of procedures in 1983, but they are still under study by the United States bishops.[33] In the meantime one case has arisen involving the investigation of a theologian's writings by the doctrinal committee of the United States bishops. Little is known about the process itself, but the final statement from the committee indicates that the dialogue was fruitful and that the theologian in question, Richard McBrien, had the right to call other theologians to defend and explain his positions.[34] Perhaps the process used in this case might prove helpful in other similar cases.

A detailed discussion of proposed guidelines lies beyond the scope of this present chapter. The major points made here are that justice and the credibility of the church's teaching office call for a recognition of the norms or criteria governing public dissent in the church, the equitable application of these norms, and the review of existing procedures to incorporate the safeguards of contemporary justice in the process of examining theologians. The call for these changes has repeatedly been made in the past. The need is even more urgent today.

In conclusion, this chapter has examined what I think are the four most signfiicant issues involved in my present dispute with the Congregation for the Doctrine of the Faith — the role of the Catholic theologian, the possibility of public theological dissent from some noninfallible hierarchical teaching, the possibility of dissent by the faithful in such cases, and the fairness of the process. The Catholic theological community needs to continue the dialogue on all these issues.

NOTES

1. All the documentation and the history of the case are found in my *Faithful Dissent* (Kansas City, MO: Sheed and Ward, 1986). Much of the documentation was also published in *Origins* 15 (1986): 665-680, 691-694.

2. John P. Boyle, "The Ordinary Magisterium: Toward a History of the Concept," *The Heythrop Journal* 20 (1979): 380-398; 21 (1980): 14-29.

3. For a discussion of all sides in the contemporary debate about morality and the hierarchical teaching office see Charles E. Curran and Richard A. McCormick, eds., *Readings in Moral Theology No. 3: The Magisterium and Morality* (New York: Paulist Press, 1982).

4. Richard A. McCormick, "L'Affaire Curran," *America* 154 (April 5, 1986): 261-267.

5. *Sapientia Christiana*, art. 27, in *Origins* 9 (June 7, 1979): 34-45.

6. John A. Alesandro, "The Rights and Responsibilities of Theologians: A Canonical Perspective," in Leo O'Donovan, ed., *Cooperation between Theologians and the Ecclesiastical Magisterium: A Report of the Joint Committee of the Canon Law Society of America and the Catholic Theological Society of America* (Washington, DC: Canon Law Society of America, 1982), pp. 106-109.

7. Jon Nilson, "The Rights and Responsibilities of Theologians: A Theological Perspective," in O'Donovan, *Cooperation between Theologians and the Ecclesiastical Magisterium*, pp. 53-75. Many contemporary theologians hold a similar position. This understanding of the role of the theologian also appears in some papers prepared for a discussion of the magisterium sponsored by the United States Bishops' Committee on Doctrine. See U.S. Bishops' Committee on Doctrine, "Report: An Ongoing Discussion of Magisterium," *Origins* 9 (1980): 541-551.

8. Alesandro in O'Donovan, "The Rights and Responsibilities of Theologians," pp. 107-109.

9. Avery Dulles, *The Resilient Church* (Garden City, NY: Doubleday, 1977), pp. 99ff.

10. John F. Hunt, Terrence R. Connelly, et al., *The Responsibility of Dissent: The Church and Academic Freedom* (New York: Sheed and Ward, 1970), pp. 23ff. This volume treats the academic and legal aspects of the defense made by myself and my colleagues at Catholic University. For the theological aspects see Charles E. Curran, Robert E. Hunt, et al., *Dissent in and for the Church* (New York: Sheed and Ward, 1970).

11. Hunt and Connelly, *The Responsibility of Dissent*, p. 39.

12. John C. Ford and Germain Grisez, "Contraception and the Infallibility of the Ordinary Magisterium," *Theological Studies* 39 (1978): 258-312.

13. Pierre Adnès, *Le Mariage* (Tournai, Belgium: Desclée, 1963), pp. 159ff.

14. Lucio Brunelli, "Interview with Cardinal Ratzinger," *National Catholic Register*, May 11, 1986, p. 5. The original interview appeared in *30 Giorni*, Maggio 1986, pp. 10, 11.

15. Francis A. Sullivan, *Magisterium: Teaching Authority in the Catholic Church* (New York: Paulist Press, 1983).

16. Curran and Hunt, *Dissent in and for the Church*, pp. 66ff.

17. National Conference of Catholic Bishops, *Human Life in Our Day* (Washington, DC: United States Catholic Conference, 1968), pp. 18, 19.

18. B. C. Butler, "Authority and the Christian Conscience," *Clergy Review* 60 (1975): 16.

19. Sullivan, *Magisterium*, pp. 159ff. Sullivan refers only to a later article by B. C. Butler, "Infallible: *Authenticum: Assensus: Obsequium*. Christian Teaching Authority and the Christian's Response," *Doctrine and Life* 31 (1981): 77-89.

20. John Thavis, "Interpretation of Dissent Could Threaten Theologians, Says Former Dean," *NC News Service*, Tuesday, May 6, 1986, pp. 19, 20.

21. James A. Coriden, Thomas J. Green, and Donald E. Heintschel, eds., *The Code of Canon Law: A Text and Commentary* (New York: Paulist Press, 1985), canon 752, p. 548.

22. Ladislas Orsy, "Reflections on the Text of a Canon," *America* 154 (May 17, 1986): 396-399.

23. Sixtus Cartechini, *De Valore Notarum Theologicarum* (Rome: Gregorian University Press, 1951).

24. E.g., Charles E. Curran, *Ongoing Revision: Studies in Moral Theology* (Notre Dame, IN: Fides Publishers, 1975), pp. 37-65; *Transition and Tradition in Moral Theology* (Notre Dame, IN: University of Notre Dame Press, 1978), pp. 43-55; *Critical Concerns in Moral Theology* (Notre Dame, IN: University of Notre Dame Press, 1984), pp. 233-256.

25. *Origins* 15 (March 27, 1986): 670.

26. McCormick, *America* 154 (April 5, 1986): 266, 267.

27. Cardinal Ratzinger emphasizes the faith of the simple faithful and the duties of the shepherds and teachers in the church to these simple faithful. See Cardinal Ratzinger, "The Church and the Theologians," *Origins* 15 (May 8, 1986): 761-770.

28. Archbishop John R. Quinn, "Norms for Church Dissent," *Origins* 4 (1974-75): 319, 320.

29. Archbishop John R. Quinn, "New Context for Contraception Teaching," *Origins* 10 (1980): 263-267.

30. Patrick Granfield, "Theological Evaluation of Current Procedures," in O'Donovan, *Cooperation between Theologians and the Ecclesiastical Magisterium*, pp. 125-132.

31. "Beschluss der Deutschen Bischofskonferenz vom 21 September 1972 zur Regelung eines Lehrbeanstandsungsverfahrens," *Archiv für katholischen Kirchenrecht* 141 (1972): 524-530.

32. *National Catholic Register*, August 12, 1984, p. 6.

33. Joint Committee of the Canon Law Society of America and the Catholic Theological Society of America, "Doctrinal Responsibilities: Procedures for Promoting Cooperation and Resolving Disputes between Bishops and Theologians," *Proceedings of the Catholic Theological Society of America* 39 (1984): 209-234.

34. U.S. Bishops' Committee on Doctrine, "Father Richard McBrien's *Catholicism*," *Origins* 15 (1985): 129-132.

2: Academic Freedom, Theology, and Catholic Institutions of Higher Learning

Academic freedom in Catholic higher education in the United States has once again become an important theoretical and practical issue. This chapter will discuss the question in three progressive stages. The first part will summarize briefly and explain the historical development which culminated in the middle 1960s with the strong endorsement of academic freedom for Catholic universities. The second part will discuss the threats to academic freedom which have recently come from new and proposed Vatican legislation. The third part will propose reasons why the Catholic Church itself should recognize the academic freedom of Catholic institutions of higher learning and of Catholic theology in these institutions.

Historical Overview and Explanation

This essay makes no pretense to propose a definite history of the relationship between Catholic higher education and academic freedom. Higher education in the United States has insisted that the college and university must be a free and autonomous center of studies with no external constraints limiting its freedom. No authority external to the university, be it lay or clerical, can make decisions which have a direct impact on the hiring, promoting, tenuring, and dismissing of faculty members. The existing literature on Catholic higher education usually points out that before 1960 it was generally accepted that Catholic higher education could not and would not accept the full American sense of academic freedom.[1] From the Catholic side the two most in-depth studies of academic freedom in the 1950s rejected the American concept of academic freedom.[2] Ecclesiastical authority, from which there is no appeal, can and should settle controversial questions in the academy. Non-Catholics also did not expect Catholic universities to accept academic freedom. Robert M. MacIver, the director of the American Academic Freedom Project housed at Columbia University, in his influential *Academic Freedom in Our Time* (1955) used statements by Catholics to illustrate the religious line of attack on academic freedom.[3]

However, in the 1960s change came quickly and somewhat dramatically. In 1965 Gerald F. Kreyche published a paper in the *National Catholic Education Association Bulletin* that called for Catholic institutions to accept full academic freedom.[4] The most evident sign of change was "The Land O'Lakes Statement" signed in 1967 by twenty-six leaders of Catholic higher education in the United States and Canada. According to this statement "To perform its teaching and research functions effectively, the Catholic university must have a true autonomy and academic freedom in the face of authority of whatever kind, lay or clerical, external to the academic community itself."[5] The changing times of the 1960s are well illustrated by the actions of the College Theology Society, which is the small professional society founded by teachers of theology in Catholic colleges. At its meeting in 1967 the society endorsed the 1940 statement of the American Association of University Professors and of the Association of American Colleges on academic freedom and tenure. However, the year before this society had defeated a motion to endorse the same statement.[6]

Since the 1960s the leaders of Catholic higher education in the United States have generally strengthened their support of and commitment to institutional autonomy and academic freedom. A very few Catholic colleges have opposed this trend.

Why this change at this time? In retrospect a number of factors influenced and helped bring about the dramatic change.

In my judgment cultural, theological, and educational factors all supported the change.

From a cultural perspective American Catholics entered into the mainstream of United States life and society in the post-World War II era. Throughout the nineteenth century and the first part of the twentieth century the Catholic Church in the United States was primarily an immigrant church. The question was often raised: Could one be both Catholic and American at the same time? Rome often feared that the Catholic Church in the United States was becoming too American and would lose its Roman Catholicism. The condemnation of Americanism in 1899 was an expression of that anxiety.[7] On the other hand, many Americans felt that Catholics could never really accept the American political and cultural ethos. The primary sticking point was the United States' emphasis on political and religious freedom. Official Catholic teaching denied religious freedom and could only tolerate as second best, and not fully endorse, the American understanding of the separation of church and state.

By the time of World War II immigration had dwindled. Catholics were patriotic supporters of their country during the war. After the war on the home scene Catholics entered more and more into the mainstream of American life and culture. On the international scene the United States and the Roman Catholic Church became the two bulwarks of the free world in the struggle against communism. Note that there is a negative aspect to all this which resulted in the failure of American Catholics at times to criticize some of their country's social conditions and its policies. However, Catholics were becoming very much at home in the United States of the 1950s.

Two events in the 1960s illustrated the fundamental compatibility between being Catholic and being American. In 1960 a Catholic, John F. Kennedy, was elected president of the United States. The conventional wisdom was that a Roman Catholic could never be elected president of the United States. Kennedy's election thus put to rest forever what had been a generally accepted axiom in American political life until that time. Roman Catholic acceptance and endorsement of the

United States political system with its emphasis on religious freedom and the separation of church and state came at the Second Vatican Council in 1965. The council's Declaration on Religious Freedom recognized the need for religious freedom.[8] Thus the chasm between being Catholic and being American was overcome. Again one must note the danger of Catholicism's losing any critical view of United States structures, ethos, and policies. The ultimate Catholic acceptance and appreciation of the principles of United States higher education with their emphasis on the autonomy of the institution and academic freedom must be seen in the light of this broader context of the relationship between being Catholic and being American.

The theological factors influencing the acceptance of academic freedom by American Catholic higher education in the 1960s are associated with developments that occurred at the Second Vatican Council (1962-1965). The most significant theological development was the already mentioned acceptance of religious freedom. No doubt Catholic thought has traditionally given more importance to order than to freedom. In the realm of political ethics Catholic teaching opposed many eighteenth- and nineteenth-century developments precisely because of their emphasis on freedom. Individualistic liberalism and freedom were the primary targets of much Catholic opposition. In the nineteenth and early twentieth century Catholics outside the English-speaking nations were strong opponents of political freedom. However, in the twentieth century the social structures changed. No longer was the threat coming from proponents of individualistic freedom, but now from the theoretical and practical tenets of totalitarianism. In the light of the new threats of fascism, nazism, and communism (with the recognition that Roman Catholicism was always more fearful of the totalitarianism from the left) Roman Catholic teaching and theology began to defend the freedom and rights of individuals. The first full-blown statement in defense of human rights in official Catholic social teaching appeared only in Pope John XXIII's 1963 encyclical *Pacem in Terris.*[9] The growing appreciation of freedom in the Catholic tradition found its greatest obstacle in the older teaching denying religious freedom. However, the Second Vatican Council was able to accept religious freedom on the basis of the dignity of the human person. In the light of the growing emphasis given to freedom in Roman Catholic self-understanding and the acceptance of religious freedom it was much easier for American Catholics to recognize the importance of and need for academic freedom.

The Second Vatican Council, in keeping with the Catholic tradition, recognized the autonomy of earthly institutions and cultures provided that autonomy is properly understood. Created things and society enjoy their own laws and values which must be developed, put to use, and regulated by human beings.[10] In this light one can more readily accept the American institutions of higher learning with their insistence on the autonomy of the institution. Catholic institutions of higher learning thus serve the church by being colleges and universities in the American sense of the term. Colleges and universities should not be changed into catechetical schools or seen merely as a continuation or extension of the pastoral teaching function of the bishops.

In the light of the Second Vatican Council the self-understanding of Catholic theology itself changed. The manualistic neo-Scholasticism, which was in vogue immediately before the Second Vatican Council, tended to see theology as an extension of the teaching role of the pope and bishops with the need to explain and confirm this teaching. However, the general theological shift at Vatican II, especially the acceptance of historical consciousness, made theology conscious of a role that did not involve merely the repetition, explanation, and defense of church teachings. The very historical process that was the experience of the Second Vatican Council showed the creative role of theology and the need for theology to constantly probe the meaning of faith in the contemporary cultural and historical circumstances. The theologians who had the greatest effect on the council had been disciplined and suspect before the council itself was convened. Theology is called to have an important role in bringing about change in Catholic thought and life.

Changes in the area of education itself also affected the

Catholic community's willingness to accept institutional autonomy and academic freedom. In 1955 John Tracy Ellis published what is now recognized as a classical essay in which he questioned the failure of Roman Catholicism to contribute to the intellectual life of the United States.[11] Many others (e.g., O'Dea; Ong) took up the challenge of this essay and explained its ramifications.[12] Catholics had been entering into leadership roles in many areas of American life, but their intellectual contribution was little or nothing. Perhaps the very fact that such a question could be raised and thoroughly discussed showed the growing maturity of American Catholicism. These discussions inevitably led to questions about Catholic higher education.

Many changes began to occur in Catholic higher education in the 1950s and 60s. Catholic colleges and universities were generally established by religious communities of women and men. The professors were often members of religious communities, and Catholic lay professors had little or no say in the functioning of the administration. The presidents and chief academic officers often were appointed by the religious community from among its own members. Boards of trustees were either nonexistent or heavily composed of members of the religious community. The college or university was often seen as an extension of the religious community and its pastoral mission.

This institutional setting gradually gave way to new and different structures by the 1970s, although some of the remnants of the older system continued to exist. In general one can describe these changes as an attempt at a greater professionalization of the role and the structure of Catholic institutions of higher learning.

Throughout the 1960s more lay people were functioning as professors and administrators. Some of these had been trained at the best American institutions of higher learning and brought with them the standards and operating procedures of the American academy. Catholic institutions began to put more emphasis on graduate study and research so that they became more conscious of the need for institutional autonomy and freedom. In striving for academic acceptability and excellence Catholic institutions were only too willing to accept the American understanding of the academy and the regulations proposed by accrediting associations. Catholic institutions wanted to be good colleges and universities.

However, Catholic college and university leaders were conscious that many American institutions of higher learning had begun as church-sponsored institutions but had ceased to have any relationship with the founding church. Catholic educators wanted their institutions of higher learning to be both Catholic and American. They frequently discussed the ways of safeguarding a Catholic identity and at the same time insisted on the academic freedom and institutional autonomy of American higher education.

Today the faculty and administration of Catholic institutions are heavily lay. The boards of trustees that run these institutions are free and independent from the founding or sponsoring religious community. Presidents in these institutions often continue to be religious or clerics, but they operate in a very different manner from the immediately post-World War II era.

What might be described as the professionalization of Catholic higher education in general also took place with regard to the teaching of theology and religion on Catholic college campuses. Theology courses were traditionally required in Catholic institutions, but before 1960 they were frequently taught by people who did not have doctoral degrees. It was often thought that the mere fact of religious profession or priestly ordination was a sufficient training for teaching theology. The first national meeting of the Society of Catholic College Teachers of Sacred Doctrine (later called the College Theology Society) was held in 1955. One of the primary concerns of this group was the poor quality of undergraduate theology courses and the need for a greater professionalization. Accrediting agencies had been critical of Catholic theology courses. The founders of this new society recognized the legitimacy of these criticisms and wanted to raise the standards of such theology and religious programs to match the standards for other faculties and courses in Catholic colleges and universities.[13]

This emphasis on a greater professionalization in Catholic higher education in general and in the teaching of theology influenced the move of Catholic higher education to accept the American academic standards and principles. All these reasons helped to explain the seemingly dramatic change which occurred in Catholic higher education in the 1960s with the acceptance of institutional autonomy and academic freedom.

Threats to Academic Freedom

No doubt the mainstream of Catholic higher education is firmly committed to academic freedom and institutional autonomy. Also ample evidence exists that the leaders of Catholic higher education in the United States have convinced the American Catholic bishops of the importance of such characteristics. In 1980 the United States Catholic bishops issued their first pastoral letter on Catholic higher education, "Catholic Higher Education and the Pastoral Mission of the Church." The letter recognizes some inevitable tensions but maintains, "Academic freedom and institutional independence in pursuit of the mission of the institution are essential components of educational quality and integrity."[14] "We shall all need to recall and to work for that 'delicate balance . . . between the autonomy of a Catholic University and the responsibilities of the hierarchy.' There need be no conflict between the two."[15]

However, the Roman Curia has been unwilling to accept the American insistence on academic freedom and institutional autonomy. These differences have come to the surface over the years in the relations between American Catholic higher education and the Vatican Congregation for Catholic Education. Three recent instances of legislation or proposed legislation for the universal church basically deny the role of institutional autonomy and academic freedom for Catholic institutions of higher learning.

In 1979 Pope John Paul II issued *Sapientia Christiana*, an apostolic constitution promulgating new norms for ecclesiastical faculties, that is, those institutions and schools that give

Vatican accredited degrees.[16] In the United States there are very few such faculties or institutions, with the department of theology at The Catholic University of America in Washington, D.C., being the best known example. According to these norms Catholic theologians in these faculties teach in the name of the church and need a canonical mission from church authorities. Church authorities existing outside the academy thus have the power to give and to withdraw this mission or license to teach.

The 1983 Code of Canon Law, proposed for the entire Latin Catholic Church, maintains in canon 812: "It is necessary that those who teach theological disciplines in any institute of higher studies have a mandate from a competent ecclesiastical authority."[17] This canon provides that a church authority, external to the academy, can and should make decisions directly involving the hiring, promoting, and dismissal of faculty in theological disciplines. At the present time it seems that this canon has not been applied in the United States, but it is definitely on the books.

Third, in April 1985 the Vatican Congregation for Catholic Education sent out a "Proposed Schema (Draft) for a Pontifical Document on Catholic Universities" containing proposed norms for all Catholic institutions of higher education throughout the world.[18] These proposed regulations build on canon 812 with its call for a competent ecclesiastical authority to give a mandate to all who teach theological disciplines in any institution of higher learning. This canon is incorporated within a broader framework emphasizing church control over these colleges and universities.

Negative reactions from the leaders of Catholic higher education to these recently proposed norms have been swift and sharp. The Association of Catholic Colleges and Universities in the United States has sharply criticized the proposed norms. The leaders of Catholic higher education in the United States are striving to keep the identity of Catholic institutions but they cannot accept the Vatican's understanding of what that identity entails. According to a report sent to the Vatican by the Association of Catholic Colleges and Universities "The real crux of the document is perceived by many to be the assertion of a power on the part of the bishops to control theologians. . . . What is proposed here is contrary to the American values of both academic freedom and due process both of which are written into most university statutes and protected by civil and constitutional law."[19]

What will happen? Will the leadership of Catholic higher education in the United States convince the Vatican Congregation for Catholic Education to change its proposed norms and allow institutional autonomy and academic freedom? Only time will tell. In the past these same leaders tried to change the proposed canon law of the church but were unsuccessful.

The present canon 812 was first proposed in the 1977 draft of the new canon law. At that time the leaders of Catholic colleges and universities in the United States strongly objected to the proposed canon and tried to have it changed. The Association of Catholic Colleges and Universities, the Catholic Theological Society of America, and a joint committee of bishops and college and university presidents all urged that the canon be deleted. Some United States and Canadian bishops tried to convince the commission for the new code to delete this canon. On April 18, 1982, delegates of the Association of Catholic Colleges and Universities met with the pope himself to try to convince him not to promulgate this canon. But the canon remained.[20]

What will happen now? Will the recently proposed norms be accepted? Will the present canon 812 begin to be applied in the United States? Only the future will give answers to these pressing questions. However, it is incumbent upon Catholic scholars to develop convincing reasons in favor of the autonomy of Catholic institutions of higher learning and of the academic freedom of such institutions, especially of Catholic theology faculties.

Defense of Academic Freedom for Catholic Institutions and for Catholic Theology

Different types of arguments can be proposed to support the need for academic freedom in Catholic institutions of higher learning and especially for the academic freedom of Catholic theology faculties. Leaders in Catholic higher education have already pointed out the practical ramifications of the proposed legislation. Such legislation in practice would probably destroy the system of Catholic higher education in the United States as we know it today. At the present time Catholic higher education receives government funding, especially in the form of grants and loans to students as well as funds for research. The Supreme Court has ruled that government funding for Catholic grammar and high schools is unconstitutional but not for Catholic colleges and universities. Catholic higher education accepts the principle of academic freedom and does not proselytize or catechize as do grammar and high schools under Catholic auspices. If the existing and proposed legislation for Catholic higher education is enforced, then the courts could very well rule unconstitutional all aid to Catholic higher education since these institutions would no longer accept the autonomy of the university and academic freedom. Thus the very existence of Catholic higher education is in jeopardy.

One cannot dismiss the significance of this practical argument. However, practical reasons should not be the primary consideration. From an ethical perspective it might be very true and necessary at times not to accept funding from other sources if this is contrary to one's own basic principles. At the very minimum the practical consideration is secondary, and a more convincing reason is needed to justify the autonomy and academic freedom of Catholic higher education. The real issue is the academic freedom of Catholic theology.

The ultimate and necessary justification for the academic freedom of Catholic institutions of higher learning and especially for Catholic theology faculties in those institutions is that such academic freedom is for the good of the church. This is the justification for academic freedom in secular society. Such freedom does not exist just for the good of certain academics and for academic institutions but is ultimately for the good of society itself and is justified precisely because of this reason.

Does academic freedom, especially that of theology, in

Catholic institutions of higher learning ultimately work for the good of the Roman Catholic Church? Can the church with an authoritative hierarchical teaching office really accept academic freedom as compatible with and even helpful for the good of the church? I believe the academic freedom of Catholic theology in institutions of higher learning is ultimately for the good of the church.

Recall what was said about the Catholic Church and Catholic theology in the previous chapter. The mission of the church is to make the word and work of Jesus present in the light of the contemporary historical and cultural circumstances. Creative fidelity must characterize the church. Creative fidelity is an apt description because the church cannot merely repeat what was said in previous generations. The word and work of Jesus must be appropriated by every age and culture.

Catholic self-understanding grounds the need for creative fidelity. The Catholic tradition has always rejected the axiom "the scripture alone." By insisting on the scripture and tradition, despite some aberrations, the Catholic self-understanding recognizes the need to make the word of God manifest in the changing situations of time and space. One cannot just cite the scripture and repeat what has been said in the past, but the word of God must be appropriated, understood, and lived in the light of the present. The early church saw the need to understand God and Jesus in the light of the Greek philosophical understanding of person and nature. Some claimed that the church could not teach there are three persons in God and two natures in Jesus because these concepts and terms are not found explicitly in the scriptures. However, the total church insisted on understanding the word of God and appropriating it in its own age.

The Catholic Church has also insisted on the importance of human reason. According to this tradition faith and reason can never contradict one another. Reason can help us to understand better our faith and the actions that spring from faith. In fact, Catholic moral teaching on specific actions has been based primarily on human reason and not directly on faith. Thus the Catholic tradition with its emphasis on scripture and tradition as well as on faith and reason insists on the characteristic of creative fidelity to the word and work of Jesus.

With this self-understanding the Roman Catholic Church has always recognized and given great significance to the role of theologians. The total church could not carry out its mission of creative fidelity without the work of theologians. Theology should be expected to be on the cutting edge of the mission of creative fidelity. Theologians will often be like the scouting party that goes out to explore before the whole group passes through. Theology prepares the way for development and the ongoing appropriation of Christian thought and action. However, some theologians will also tend to stress the fidelity aspect and will be very cautious about new developments. There is no one role for theology in general to play, but the work of theologians is necessary for the total mission of creative fidelity of the church itself.

However, what is characteristic of Roman Catholicism is the role of the hierarchical teaching office in the church. It is precisely because of the existence of an authoritative teaching office in the church that many would argue against the legitimacy of academic freedom for Catholic theologians. But it is important to understand how the authoritative teaching office of pope and bishops functions.

First, the authoritative teaching office or magisterium is itself subject to the word of God and the truth, as is seen in the Constitution on Divine Revelation of Vatican II (n. 10). This teaching authority with the help of the Holy Spirit discerns the truth and the word of God. This understanding coheres with the basic Catholic tradition that morality is intrinsic. Something is commanded because it is true and good and not the other way around. Authority must conform itself to the truth.

Second, there are different levels of authoritative church teaching. Some teachings are by their nature core and central to the faith, whereas other teachings are more removed from the core of faith. Contemporary Catholic ecclesiology and canon law accept the distinction between infallible teaching which calls for an assent of faith on the part of the faithful and authoritative, noninfallible teaching which demands the religious respect of intellect and will. Even in infallible teaching Catholic self-understanding recognizes the possibility and even the need to deepen, improve, and develop the teaching, which is one of the functions of theologians. Noninfallible teachings according to a document of the German bishops "involve a certain element of the provisional even to the point of being capable of including error."[21] It is generally accepted that such authoritative, noninfallible teaching enjoys a presumption of truth in its favor. However, such teaching has been wrong in the past, and the presumption always cedes to the truth. Thus, all must recognize that the role of Catholic theology is not merely to repeat and defend official church formulations.

Third, the hierarchical teaching office is not identical with the total teaching function of the church. The primary teacher in the church is the Holy Spirit. All the baptized share in the teaching role of Jesus just as they share in the priestly role, but there still exists a hierarchical teaching function and a hierarchical priestly function. Such a view does not claim that the church is a democracy, but it does recognize a pluralistic theory of teaching authorities which can and should serve as mutual checks and balances.

Fourth, the pastoral role of the hierarchical teaching office and the teaching function of theologians are somewhat independent and cooperative. The hierarchical teaching function is conferred with an office in the church and has the promise of the assistance of the Holy Spirit to discern the truth. The theological teaching function rests on the faithful scholarship of the individual and the community of scholars. The theologians' teaching function is not merely derivative from or an extension of the hierarchical teaching office. Yes, the theologian must give due assent to official hierarchical teaching, but the teaching role of the theologian differs from the pastoral teaching role of pope and bishops.

Fifth, history reminds us of the existence and importance of the somewhat independent and cooperative teaching role of theologians. The apostolic church gives a distinct role to *didaskoloi* who teach in their own right and not merely as delegates of the *episkopoi* or *presbyteroi*. In the Middle Ages there was a magisterium of doctors or theologians in the church. The term magisterium referred primarily to theologians and not to pastors. Theological faculties exercised an independent teaching authority. In some ecumenical councils theologians had a deliberative vote. Even at the Second Vatican Council the somewhat independent and cooperative role of theologians stands out when one studies what the council accomplished.

In this connection it should be noted that the understanding of the role of the theologian proposed here does not confuse the role of the theologian with that of the pastoral teaching office in the church. The teaching office of pope and bishops deserves a respect which of itself is not due to the teaching of theologians. To the pastoral teaching office of pope and bishops even in noninfallible matters one owes a religious respect of intellect and will. However, it still could be that noninfallible teachings are erroneous and that infallible teachings need to be improved and deepened. Likewise, such an understanding does not call for two magisteria in the church but recognizes the role and limitations of the official hierarchical teaching office.

In the United States context the academic freedom of the academic theologian is a very legitimate way to safeguard the somewhat independent and cooperative role of the theologian in the teaching function of the Roman Catholic Church. But what about the mistakes that theologians will make? It is inevitable that theologians will make mistakes, but there are three important safeguards to protect against the mistakes that will be made.

First, theological debate, like all scholarly debate, seeks the truth. In the critique and give-and-take of theological discussion one hopes to come to the truth. Such discussion and mutual criticism constitute the means that the academy itself presents to help safeguard the search for truth. The Catholic Church has known vigorous theological debate over the years. In fact, at times that debate has gone too far and offended against Christian charity and even the unity of the church. Manuals of theology even acknowledged a special type of hatred — *odium theologicum*: theological hatred — because of the vehemence with which some theological debates have been carried on in the church.

A second safeguard against the danger of theological mistakes and abuses is found in the right of the hierarchical magisterium to point out what it judges to be theological error and ambiguity. At times the hierarchical magisterium may judge that such interventions are necessary to safeguard faith. All have to recognize that this could be a necessary and apt use of the hierarchical teaching office. In pointing out the errors and ambiguities of a theology or of a particular theologian this action of the hierarchical magisterium would have no direct effect on the role of the individual theologian in the academy. Academic freedom means that no external authority, lay or clerical, can make decisions affecting the hiring, promoting, tenuring, and dismissing of faculty members. However, the hierarchical teaching office can safeguard the faith of its members through such an intervention if it deems it necessary and helpful.

A third safeguard against theological mistakes and abuses is found in the recognized academic norm that even a tenured professor can be dismissed for incompetency, but the judgment of incompetency must be made by academic peers in accord with academic due process. Competency demands that a Catholic theologian theologize within the Catholic faith parameters. A Catholic theologian who does not believe in Jesus or does not accept a role for the pope in the church could rightly be judged to be incompetent. However, this judgment must be made by academic peers and in accord with academic due process and not by church authorities external to the academy.

There will never be a perfect solution to the tensions between the role of the hierarchical teaching office and the role of the theologian. The tension between these roles is rooted ultimately in the tension of creative fidelity to the word and work of Jesus which is the characteristic mission of the whole church. A living church and a living tradition will always know and experience tensions.

Theology is necessary for the life of the church, and it serves the church in general and the hierarchical teaching office itself. Academic freedom protects the role of some theologians and gives them the freedom to make their necessary contribution to the life of the church. Theologians will make mistakes and might even abuse this academic freedom, but safeguards exist to protect against the damage that such mistakes might cause the church. The academic freedom of the academic theologian in the long run is good not only for the church but for the hierarchical teaching office in the church. The teaching office will be more credible in the light of the recognition of the academic freedom of Catholic theologians.

The academic freedom of Catholic theologians and of Catholic colleges and universities must ultimately be justified as being for the good of the church itself. This section has attempted to make such a case for academic freedom. I think the vast majority of Catholic theologians writing today would agree with the role of theology described here. However, at the present time official church documents and legislation do not seem to be willing to accept this role of the Catholic theologian as proposed here. In the midst of these tensions it is all the more necessary to develop and to strengthen the arguments for the acceptance of the academic freedom of Catholic theology and of Catholic institutions of higher learning on the basis of their contribution to the good of the Catholic Church itself.

NOTES

1. Philip Gleason, "Academic Freedom: Survey, Retrospect, and Prospects," *National Catholic Education Association Bulletin* 64 (1967): 67-74; Gleason, "Academic Freedom and the Crisis in Catholic Universities," in Edward Manier and John W. Houck, eds., *Academic Freedom and the Catholic University* (Notre Dame, IN: Fides, 1967), pp. 33-56; Gleason, "Freedom and the Catholic University," *National Catholic Education Association Bulletin* 65 (1968): 21-29.

2. Charles Donahue, "Freedom and Education: The Pluralistic Background," *Thought* 27 (1952-53): 542-560; Donahue, "Freedom and Education: The Sacral Problem," *Thought* 28 (1953-54): 209-223; Donahue, "Freedom and Education, III: Catholicism and Academic Freedom," *Thought* 29 (1954-55): 555-573; Aldo J. Tos, "A Critical Study of American Views on Academic Freedom" (Ph.D. dissertation, The Catholic University of America, 1958).

3. Robert M. MacIver, *Academic Freedom in Our Time* (New York: Columbia University Press, 1955), pp. 134-146.

4. Gerard F. Kreyche, "American Catholic Higher Education

and Academic Freedom," *National Catholic Education Association Bulletin* 65 (1968): 21-29.

5. "Land O'Lakes Statement," in Neil G. McCluskey, ed., *The Catholic University: A Modern Appraisal* (Notre Dame, IN: University of Notre Dame Press, 1970), p. 336.

6. Rosemary Rodgers, *A History of the College Theology Society* (Villanova, PA: The College Theology Society, 1983), pp. 28-30.

7. Thomas T. McAvoy, *The Americanist Heresy in Roman Catholicism* (Notre Dame, IN: University of Notre Dame Press, 1963).

8. Richard J. Reagan, *Conflict and Consensus: Religious Freedom and the Second Vatican Council* (New York: Macmillan, 1967).

9. Pope John XXIII, *Pacem in Terris*, in David J. O'Brien and Thomas A. Shannon, eds., *Renewing the Earth: Catholic Documents on Peace, Justice and Liberation* (Garden City, NY: Doubleday Image Books, 1977), nn. 11-27, pp. 126-130.

10. *Gaudium et Spes*, The Pastoral Constitution on the Church in the Modern World, in O'Brien and Shannon, *Renewing the Earth*, n. 41, p. 215; n. 59, pp. 237-238.

11. John Tracy Ellis, "American Catholicism and the Intellectual Life," *Thought* 30 (1955-56): 351-388.

12. Thomas F. O'Dea, *American Catholic Dilemma: An Inquiry into the Intellectual Life* (New York: Sheed and Ward, 1958); Walter J. Ong, *Frontiers in American Catholicism* (New York: Macmillan, 1957).

13. Rodgers, *A History of the College Theology Society*, pp. 11-20.

14. United States Catholic Bishops, "Pastoral Letter: Catholic Higher Education and the Church's Pastoral Mission," *Origins* 10 (1980): 380.

15. Ibid., p. 381.

16. Pope John Paul II, *Sapientia Christiana*, *Origins* 9 (1979): 34-45.

17. James A. Coriden, "The Teaching Office in the Church," in James A. Coriden, Thomas J. Green, and Donald E. Heintschel, eds., *The Code of Canon Law: Text and Commentary* (New York: Paulist Press, 1985), p. 575.

18. Congregation of Catholic Education, "Proposed Schema (Draft) for a Pontifical Document on Catholic Universities," *Origins* 15 (1986): 706-711.

19. Association of Catholic Colleges and Universities, "Catholic College Presidents Respond to Proposed Vatican Schema," *Origins* 15 (1986): 703.

20. Coriden, *The Code of Canon Law: Text and Commentary*, pp. 575, 576.

21. Cited at length in Karl Rahner, *Theological Investigations*, vol. XIV: *Ecclesiology, Questions in the Church, the Church in the World* (New York: Seabury Press, 1976), p. 86.

3: Personal Reaction and Response

In August 1979 I was informed that I was under investigation by the Congregation for the Doctrine of the Faith because of my writings in moral theology, especially in the area of sexuality. After, in my judgment, a very unsatisfactory process and dialogue, Cardinal Joseph Ratzinger, the prefect of the congregation, in a September 17, 1985, letter invited me "to reconsider and to retract those positions which violate the conditions necessary for a professor to be called a Catholic theologian." I declined.

I have always recognized that my nuanced and qualified positions on the issues involved — contraception, sterilization, abortion, euthanasia, masturbation, premarital intercourse, homosexual acts, the possibility of divorce and remarriage — were in dissent from the official, noninfallible hierarchical teaching. Recent literature shows that the vast majority of Catholic theologians maintain the legitimacy of and need for public theological dissent on these issues. This chapter will not attempt to prove the truth or legitimacy of my opinions; rather, my present concern is to address some questions which I have proposed to myself and others have raised.

A Teaching Moment

I arrived at my positions after much study, dialogue, searching, and prayer. In conscience I could not change them. Beginning in October 1985 I met with Archbishop James A. Hickey, the chancellor of The Catholic University of America, and Cardinal Joseph Bernardin, the chair of the board of trustees, on four different occasions and suggested a possible compromise. Earlier I had proposed a different compromise. On January 16, 1986, Archbishop Hickey informed me that the later compromise was not acceptable. The congregation had already made its decisions and judgments, but Cardinal Ratzinger would be willing, if I requested it, to receive me in an informal, private meeting. We agreed to such a private meeting with a joint press release after the meeting. This session took place at the Vatican on March 8, 1986. Later that afternoon the congregation released our bland joint statement announcing that our meeting had taken place.

What to do? What was clear to me was the opportunity to use this occasion as a teaching moment. Since I have been teaching Catholic theology since 1961 and have been a member of the department of theology of The Catholic University of America since 1965, I wanted to use this occasion to carry on my teaching vocation. In my judgment such continued teaching on these issues of dissent was for the ultimate good of the church.

After my meeting at the Vatican, despite some optimistic moments, I remained generally convinced that the congregation would ultimately take action against me. Archbishop Hickey had told me that in such a case he would move to take away my canonical mission to teach theology in the ecclesiastical faculty of theology at The Catholic University of America. I was convinced then that I would probably lose in the short term, but I was more concerned about the long term.

From my first public comments I insisted on the goal of making the whole affair a teaching moment. I wanted to concentrate on three areas: the possibility of public dissent by theologians in theory and by the faithful in practice from some noninfallible church teaching; the need for the church to change its teaching in these areas for its own good and its own credibility; and the role of the Catholic university in its service to the truth and to the church.

This goal affects not only what I have tried to do but also how I have tried to do it. As a teacher one strives to present carefully and objectively all aspects of an issue and then chooses one's own position and gives reasons for it. I think it is always important to avoid attributing motives to people, name-calling, and angry rhetoric that detract from the reasonable debate that should take place. In this particular teaching moment I also wanted to model how discussion and even dissent should take place within the community of the Roman Catholic Church. Often in the last year I have cited as my way of proceeding the age old axiom *in necessariis unitas, in dubiis libertas, in omnibus caritas* — in necessary matters, unity; in doubtful matters, freedom; in all things, charity. The church as the community of the disciples of Jesus cannot and should not agree on all issues, but disagreement and discussion should take place in an atmosphere of respect for all concerned.

As I reflected on the possibility of using this whole occasion as a teaching moment in and for the church, some questions came to mind. What if I am wrong? If I speak out, will this hurt some people in the church who will not understand what I am trying to do?

As a scholar I recognize the threats to objectivity from my own perspective and prejudices. I hope that I can truly be open so that I can change my positions when confronted by evidence for a change. At the present time the support of so many colleagues has corroborated my own judgment on the legitimacy and need for such public theological dissent, but even so I could be wrong. In that case the church would still gain by the open discussion that has taken place. The glory of the Catholic theological tradition, especially in moral theology, has been the acceptance of the goodness of the human and of human reason. Faith and reason can never contradict one another. Such discussion, even if I were proved to be wrong, would still benefit the church.

Undoubtedly some people in the church, especially those who see the pre-Vatican II model as normative, are upset and hurt by my continued public dissent. For them the role of the theologian is to expound loyally all and only what the hierarchical magisterium has said. One has to recognize the differences existing within the Catholic Church. Chapter one has discussed the two different understandings of the role of the theologians in the church today. Accordingly, I am aware that some Catholics are truly perplexed and troubled by my actions. But education is what is needed. The Catholic Church must recognize the legitimacy of public theological dissent and even hold open the possibility of changing its teachings on the issues concerned. As a teacher I try to work for such changes, while avoiding any personal attacks on those who disagree with me. By the manner of my teaching I try not to exacerbate the already existing tension, for I recognize that in the church we must be able to disagree on nonfundamental aspects without sundering the unity that makes us a community.

But there was even a stronger objection to my making this occasion a teaching moment. Would it not have been better to remain silent and say nothing about the issues? I wrestled with this objection at the time, and a number of people have raised the same objection in private and in public. Many of the theological leaders of Vatican II — Yves Congar, John Courtney Murray, Henri de Lubac — had been disciplined by the church before the council, but they accepted their discipline and remained silent. Some people in the United States reminded me especially of the example of John Courtney Murray, who quietly withdrew from the study of and writing on church-state relations after he was "silenced." In the end history and Vatican II vindicated him. Was silence not the proper way to go?

I was very conscious of this objection. In an earlier small book on priestly ministry published in 1972 I wrote about the spirituality of the paschal mystery and used Yves Congar as a contemporary example of one who suffered at the hands of the church. Congar was greatly restricted in his teaching and his writing, but he silently endured everything and said nothing at the time. While praising Congar's approach, I raised the question about the possibility of his having taken a different approach.

In my case a number of factors influenced my rejection of the option of silence and passive acceptance of the action against me. First of all I have not been silenced by religious superiors. My situation is quite different. The action taken against me was the judgment that I am neither suitable nor eligible to be a professor of Catholic theology. I have not been silenced. As will be developed later, I had a right to a public hearing of my case.

Second, the issues involved in the controversy are issues that every Catholic family in the United States and the world is facing one way or another. Questions of personal sexuality are not the primary issues or aspects of the Christian life, and there is the danger that we in the United States will concentrate on these questions and forget the more important realities of justice facing our society and our world. However, these questions remain real problems and issues for the people involved and call for continued discussion.

As a theologian I have always been willing to admit that I have learned from the experience of Christian people. This experience cannot be absolutized and it must always be criticized, but it is a source of theological knowledge (*locus theologicus*). I see one of the roles of theologians as articulating this experience and trying to insert it into the ongoing tradition of Catholic theology and life. Many Catholics who have become frustrated with the teaching of the church on these issues have been somewhat comforted by the fact that theologians are calling for a reconsideration of the official teaching in these areas. As a theologian who has received tremendous support from so many people I have felt a continuing obligation to articulate and voice their experience.

At the same time, according to sociological studies many Catholics have left the church because of the official hierarchical teaching on questions of artificial contraception and other issues. In my judgment it is very important to point out that one can disagree on these issues and still remain a loyal Roman Catholic. This teaching moment would help to make clear to many Catholics the legitimacy of such dissent and the fact that they do not have to leave the church because they disagree in theory and in practice on these issues. In this context it is especially important to carry on the dissent in a respectful and charitable manner.

Third, the circumstances have changed greatly since pre-Vatican II times. Pope Paul VI even referred to "the lively debate" that followed his encyclical *Humanae Vitae* condemning artificial contraception. The very credibility of the teaching of the church is enhanced if people know there is room for dialogue and discussion within the church itself. Many Roman Catholics would be totally disenchanted if such a discussion and debate could not take place.

Fourth, my case differs from the others because it concerns the university as an institution in the service of society and the church. I am not merely an isolated individual in this issue. The nature and function of catholic universities in general and The Catholic University of America in particular are intimately a part of the question. The previous chapter has considered in great detail the issues facing Catholic higher education in the light of recent and proposed Vatican actions. The present discussion focuses only on why I decided not to remain silent about my case.

"The Canonical Statutes for the Ecclesiastical Faculties of The Catholic University" were approved in 1981 in accord with the Apostolic Constitution *Sapientia Christiana*. According to these statutes the chancellor of the university, who is the archbishop of Washington, can withdraw the canonical mission to teach in an ecclesiastical faculty only for the most serious reasons. The member of the faculty in question can ask for the due-process procedures according to which a faculty committee is to conduct a hearing to determine if the chancellor has the most serious reasons to withdraw the canonical mission. However, according to this process the final decision is to be made by the board of trustees. I had a right to this process, but I did not have to take advantage of it. In August 1986 I faced the question of what to do.

Most people I consulted advised me that in the end I probably would not win the case because the board of trustees would side with the chancellor, and the final decision rested with them. The process would inevitably drag on for at least a year and consume a large measure of my time and energy. Why waste this year if the trustees would probably rule against me? In addition, this process as such was not necessary to achieve my goal of a teaching moment. However, I decided to accept the process and go through with it. Why?

Three reasons contributed to my decision. First, my colleagues requested me to accept the process. On August 1 Dean William Cenkner of the School of Religious Studies informed me by letter that the school's Committee on Academic Freedom and Procedures by a formal vote urged me to opt for the process but recognized that my "physical and mental health must always take priority." I discussed this letter with the dean, the chair of theology, and some other faculty who were present in the month of August.

I wanted to discuss and air thoroughly all the possible consequences. If I would ultimately lose in this process, why go through with it? Would such a result not harm the theological enterprise at Catholic University even more? A very logical result of initiating this due-process procedure might be the need to move to the civil court if the university were not to follow its own statutes or were to violate my valid civil contract as a tenured professor in the department of theology. Would this legal process be a good thing? I knew there were some colleagues who disagreed with my position and denied its legitimacy. Would the resulting disagreements and tensions be harmful and destructive for the department of theology and the Catholic University? Would it be better for all concerned if I just remained silent and did not go through with the process?

However, the general response was firmly in favor of my asking for the process. If my canonical mission could be removed by the Vatican and the chancellor, the reputation and the very academic existence of the department of theology were threatened. It would be obvious there was no academic freedom at Catholic University, and there really was not a university department of theology. At most it would be a catechetical or a propaganda institute which would not attract outstanding faculty or graduate students. Many of the better faculty members at the present time would sorely be tempted to go elsewhere in the future. Some colleagues thought that the trustees would find it difficult to go against a faculty committee decision in my favor. These arguments of the dean and my colleagues were somewhat persuasive, although I personally was still very pessimistic about the final outcome. I appreciated the support that so many of my faculty had given me, and I wanted to be open to their requests and urging. In addition there were other strong reasons for my asking for the process.

The due process itself, for a second reason, continues the teaching moment. In a public way I can now make my case that theological dissent from some noninfallible hierarchical teaching is legitimate. As a matter of fact even before the hearings had begun, the teaching moment came to life. The boards of directors of both the Catholic Theological Society of America and the College Theology Society unanimously submitted testimony to the hearing committee of faculty peers defending the theological legitimacy of what I have said and done. These societies have asked their members, both individually and corporately as faculties, to submit their own testimony to the inquiry committee. A surprisingly large number have responded to this request. Thus, even before the official hearing began, the theological community in North America continued the teaching moment.

A third and very important reason to pursue the process within the university with all the means at my disposal comes from my commitment to the academic freedom of Catholic universities in general and of The Catholic University of America in particular. I have written extensively on academic freedom. In addition, in the 1968-69 school year, together with my colleagues at Catholic University who dissented from the encyclical *Humanae Vitae*, I went through an academic hearing by a board of faculty peers to determine if by our declarations and actions in dissenting from *Humanae Vitae* we had violated our responsibility as Catholic scholars at The Catholic University of America. The inquiry process took one academic year. The faculty board of inquiry concluded that our declarations and actions were responsible.

The decision was hailed as a landmark case. It proved that even at The Catholic University of America true academic freedom should and does exist and that Catholic theologians can responsibly dissent from some noninfallible hierarchical church teachings. I personally appreciated the help and support of so many people during that hearing, especially our legal counsel, John F. Hunt and Terrence Connelly of the

New York firm of Cravath, Swaine, and Moore. One of my strongest reasons for staying at Catholic University all these years was appreciation for the many people on campus and off campus who had supported me at that time as well as in the matter of my firing which had occurred in 1967.

But in August 1986 the situation was dramatically different. If I could be removed by the Vatican congregation and the chancellor from teaching theology at The Catholic University of America, then there was no academic freedom and institutional autonomy in that institution. Since in theory and in practice I had expended so much time and energy affirming and promoting academic freedom for Catholic institutions of higher learning and especially for Catholic University, it seemed appropriate to continue the struggle until there were no other means available.

Thus the teaching moment continues. No matter what happens I will continue to address the question of public dissent, the issues involved in my case, and academic freedom, but there are many other questions that I want to explore and research. I am eager to continue my work as a Catholic moral theologian on the broad front of all the problems and issues in the field. However, a more basic question has been raised and needs an answer.

Why Am I Still a Roman Catholic?

Many people both within and outside the Roman Catholic Church have asked me why I am still a Roman Catholic. This is a very significant and deeply personal question which I have been facing in the light of the recent Vatican action taken against me. Ever since the process with Rome began in 1979 there was the possibility that the Congregation for the Doctrine of the Faith might condemn my theology and take action against me. By 1984 I was convinced that the process would not turn out well. Now I have been declared by the highest authority in my church to be neither suitable nor eligible to teach Catholic theology.

Without doubt such an action constitutes a rejection of the

vocation I have followed as a Roman Catholic theologian. Since 1961 I have been teaching and studying Catholic moral theology. In this capacity I have lived in the two worlds of the academy and the church. For me the church aspect of my work has been the most significant. For this reason I have taught at Catholic University for over twenty years because here I could have an important influence on the theology and life of the church. Despite offers and opportunities to go elsewhere and despite some tensions within the institution I decided to stay at Catholic University. Now the Congregation for the Doctrine of the Faith with the approval of the pope has repudiated my theology.

Such action is bound to have personal effects. There is no doubt that I have felt hurt by this action. In my judgment the action taken against me is wrong. Above all the injustice of the Vatican declaration has seemed obvious. All theologians recognize that many others hold positions similar to mine. Cardinal Ratzinger, the prefect of the congregation, and the Roman authorities cannot be ignorant of this fact. The entire process itself seemed to lack the judicial requirements for guaranteeing my rights, and at the same time our written correspondence indicates, in the words of another author, that the congregation's response to me was stonewalling.

However, my hurt must be put into proper perspective. In fact there are a number of perspectives that help to explain my continuing commitment to the Roman Catholic Church — the personal, the ecclesiological, and the theological.

Personal Perspectives

We all have different personalities and character traits. I have been amazed at the depth of reaction of many people to the Vatican's action taken against me. People have told me of their anger, frustration, depression, tears, and sleepless nights. I have experienced these to some limited degree but not to the extent mentioned to me by many friends and colleagues.

My personality obviously affects how I have responded. I am not one to dwell on the past or on past hurts. I tend to forget about the past and move on to the future. There is a curious combination of realism and optimism about me. I am realistic enough to know that often I cannot really change things, and there is no sense wasting time and effort in what cannot be changed. Moreover, I feel that there will be opportunities in the future to do things that I could not have done in my present position. My Christian faith as well as my historical experience reinforces these feelings.

Many things have happened to me in life that have not been of my own choosing, but I have adapted well to them and have been quite content. Yes, I did choose to become a Catholic priest, but I really did not choose to become a professor or a moral theologian. My bishop assigned me to study and ultimately to teach moral theology. I never saw myself as a university professor, but this possibility became real after I was told that I could no longer teach in the diocesan seminary. Even my own writing has been in response to the needs of the life of the church and the discipline of moral theology. Perhaps at times I have allowed outside events and forces to exercise too much control on me, but such an attitude has made it much easier for me to cope with the present situation.

In addition there is the need to put into proper perspective exactly what Rome has done to me. No one has said that I am no longer a member of the church. In no way have I been excommunicated. No action has been taken against me as a priest. I am realistic enough to know that such a possibility always exists and in other circumstances might have been a reality in my case. Church authority has only declared that I am no longer suitable nor eligible to be a Catholic theologian. This will probably cost me my teaching job at the department of theology at Catholic University and will probably restrict where I can teach in the future. However, most people have had the same experience of losing a job.

Even in the matter of being a Catholic theologian the action by the Congregation for the Doctrine of the Faith will by no means have catastrophic effects. I am reasonably confident that I will be able to find good teaching opportunities in the area of my specialty.

In a very true sense the Vatican action has provided me

a much greater audience than I ever would have had before. One newspaper cartoon showed the pope announcing that he was silencing an American theologian. The next picture in the cartoon showed me surrounded by banks of microphones. My influence as a teacher is infinitely greater as a result of the Vatican action. The challenge is for me to take advantage responsibly of this opportunity to continue my teaching function. In all my reactions to the Vatican action I have stressed my intention to make the whole situation a teaching moment.

In all honesty the Vatican declaration against me has not hurt my reputation as a theologian. Despite the congregation's action the overwhelming majority of my colleagues have supported me. I have felt both grateful and humbled by that response. My peers have been loud in their praise and courageous in their willingness to speak out in support of me. The whole world knows that I am a competent and respected Catholic moral theologian.

Yes, there is some hurt and some suffering in all this for me, but these negative aspects pale in comparison with what so many other people suffer and endure. I have had very little suffering in my life. I am constantly amazed at the courage and strength shown by so many people whom I know and others whom I have never met. We are all aware of the vast majority of human beings who suffer from hunger and starvation, who lack the basic necessities for a minimally decent human existence, and who suffer oppression in many forms. Also I think of all the physical and psychic suffering in the world—the problems of the handicapped, the oppressed, those committed to various institutions. I marvel at the strength and resiliency of parents who have handicapped children. So many people have been deeply hurt and wounded in their different human relationships, but I have been supported by so many friends and others. The only thing that has happened to me is that I have lost a job.

Yes, there is some added hurt that arises from the fact that the wrong comes from those who should give support and encouragement. However, within the church many have suffered much more than I. I think of all those people who have to deal personally and existentially with the problems that I have been dealing with from a more theoretical perspective. I know other theologians who have lost their teaching posts, especially in seminaries, because of the positions they have taken. Such people have not had the advantage I have had of strong public support from colleagues and others. Above all I can appreciate the pain and anguish of many women within the Roman Catholic Church at the present time. The alienation of Catholic women is readily understandable. In the last few years I have learned much from my women students as they have experienced these problems. Their theological understandings have made them more conscious of the discrimination against women in the church. Some have decided after great pain that they had to leave the church. Others are clinging to the church by recognizing the need for moral support from outside official church structures. Others are determined to continue their struggle to change the church no matter what the price.

From both theoretical and practical viewpoints I have seen the spirituality of the paschal mystery as central in the Christian life. The mystery of dying and rising is at the heart of Christian belief and of Christian discipleship. The problems of evil and of suffering raise troubling questions for all of us. Christian faith has no easy escape from these problems, but the life, death, and resurrection of Jesus shed light on the meaning of human suffering. The moral imperative of our baptism calls for us to suffer, to die, and to rise with Jesus. Especially in the context of the paschal mystery my sufferings are very small in comparison with the problems of so many others.

Thus from a number of different personal perspectives the Vatican action against me is not all that harmful and distressing. In fact great good even for me has come about because of this action against me.

Ecclesial Perspectives

My differences with the official hierarchical teaching are well known, but these differences constitute only one com-

paratively small part of my relationship with the church. First
of all I have continuously emphasized that my disagreements
are in areas that are not core and central to the faith. For this
reason my dispute does not really go to the heart and center
of Christian faith in the Catholic tradition. I have been standing up for one's right to disagree on these matters and still
be a loyal Roman Catholic. Consequently, in my own life
I can certainly continue to be a committed Roman Catholic
and have these differences.

The core matters of faith are very significant and important for me personally. God's loving relationship in covenant
with human beings through Jesus and the Spirit gives intelli-
gibility to human existence and the human enterprise. We
do not live only for ourselves but for one another within this
community of believers. We have been created by God and
redeemed by Jesus in the power of the Spirit. This loving gift
of God calls for my commitment and response. Human existence is not just a time to acquire what I can for myself.
Material goods are not the most important matters. In the
last analysis the most important things are human persons,
but the fullness of the human person only can come to its
flowering in the light of faith and empowerment by God.

Life for me would be void and empty if there were not this
ultimate religious dimension to it. The life, death, and resurrection of Jesus say something very important about my own
life, death, and resurrection. In the midst of human existence
there are no easy answers to the questions we face, and there
are no shortcuts in living out our existence. However, the
power and presence of the Spirit within the community of the
disciples of Jesus give me great strength and hope. It is important for me to participate in the Eucharistic celebrations
of the community of the disciples of Jesus and to be both consoled and challenged by that community.

Even within the context of the practical issues facing human
existence and the life of the church the matters involved in
my dispute with Rome are not the most important issues.
From a Christian perspective the questions of justice, peace,
truth, love, freedom, and personal integrity will always remain the primary issues. I am always worried that the sexual

questions can be an escape from the more important issues. A preoccupation with sexual matters can well represent the typical bourgeois mentality. However, even though these issues are not the most important ones, they are significant matters that must be faced by all people. In addition, these issues have occasioned much anguish and suffering for many people in the church.

Dissent on these noninfallible questions in the theological and ecclesial realms can be compared to civil disobedience in the civic sphere. Civil disobedience is not revolution. The revolutionary believes that the entire system is unjust and must be overturned. However, one engages in civil disobedience to protest and to try to change one aspect or element within a system to which one is committed and which is basically just. Civil disobedience very often calls for society to live up to its own principles in areas where it has failed to do so. Martin Luther King, Jr., well exemplified this understanding of civil disobedience. So too dissent from noninfallible church teaching is not revolution nor motivated by a break with the church. The dissenter is committed to the church and is trying to bring about change for the good of the church itself.

The danger exists that the dissenter will become so absorbed by the dissent that one can readily become estranged from the church in the more significant areas. The dissenter who has been disciplined in some way by church authority must be careful not to succumb to the temptation of seeing only opposition between oneself and the total church. Opposition to church authority can readily grow and become more than just dissent from noninfallible teaching. The dissenter must keep all things in proper perspective.

In the midst of my struggle I have constantly stressed the importance of transcendence, which is the more technical and philosophical name I give to the need to keep things in their proper perspective. Transcendence should give one the proper distance from one's own immediate preoccupations. As a believer I think there are three important attitudes that help to make transcendence a reality — prayer, humor, and forgiveness. Transcendence brings about distancing from the nitty gritty and the problems of the present. Prayer is a very traditional practical implementation of the reality of transcendence. In prayer one transcends without in any way denying the problems of the present. Humor is another great sign and means of implementing transcendence. To laugh at oneself is a very important way of putting distance between oneself and the problems of the present. The Christian gospel calls for the need to forgive. Forgiveness is the ability to go beyond one's present difficulties and not to be entrapped in them. Forgiveness calls for a bigness of heart and soul that allows one to transcend the predicament of the moment. Prayer, humor, and forgiveness can be called in a true sense the strategies of transcendence that allow the dissenter in the church to keep one's own dissent in proper perspective within a relationship of continuing commitment to the church. In practice I have tried in the manner and mode of my dissent to make sure that such dissent is seen within the context of my love for and commitment to the church. A very important ecclesiological perspective is the recognition that my dissent is on more remote and peripheral matters and coexists within a context of assent as well as commitment to the church.

A second important ecclesiological perspective concerns the notion of the church as the people of God. Many have often raised the question "How do you feel about being rejected by your own church?" As mentioned earlier, I have not been rejected as a member of the church or even as a priestly minister. Rome has disagreed only with my theological positions. However, Rome is not the whole church. I have been supported and sustained by so many in the church who have truly ministered to me in the midst of my present dispute. I have heard from many people I have not seen in decades. Strangers have written me hundreds of letters of support. People who attended a workshop or a talk have written to express their concern and support. Many groups, especially religious communities of women, have written me official letters of encouragement and solidarity.

It is impossible to mention by name all the people in the church who have encouraged me, but a few categories come to mind. First of all my students. Present and former students have been very vocal in their support for me. Many have written letters or articles defending me in the press. At Catholic University a group of students formed Friends of American Catholic Theology (FACT) to work for my support. They organized and executed ways of disseminating the facts of my case and of garnering support for me. Theological colleagues within and outside Catholic University have signed statements on my behalf and come to my support in different ways. The board of directors of both the Catholic Theological Society of America and the College Theology Society unanimously passed long letters of support for me as a Roman Catholic theologian and objected to any efforts to prevent my teaching in such a capacity. A great number of these theologians publicly supported me in the knowledge that such actions might jeopardize their own careers. In no way do I feel rejected by my church. I have received so much solidarity, concern, and support from so many people in the church.

In this context a brief word should be said about the support of non-Catholic colleagues in Christian ethics and theology. As one might expect, they have been very sympathetic to me and my positions, but there has been a general and genuine feeling that the action against me has hurt the Catholic Church and Christianity as a whole. These non-Catholic colleagues are not gloating over the predicament of the church but only saddened and concerned about the problem.

A third ecclesiological perspective for understanding my situation is the historical aspect. I have always been interested in history and continue to insist that we can learn much from it. History has helped me to understand better the work and the tensions of being a theologian in the Catholic Church.

To its credit Roman Catholicism has always taken the role of theology very seriously. One Protestant colleague consoled me with the thought that at least my church takes its theologians seriously. His church shows little or no interest in what he says and writes. Theologians in the Catholic tradition have always played a significant role in the explanation and development of church teaching.

The whole church is called to creative fidelity to the word and work of Jesus. History shows that the church has tried to understand, appropriate, and live this in the light of changing historical and cultural circumstances. Facing new situations requires new understandings and developments. Thus, in the early days of the church questions very quickly arose about admitting Gentiles to the community and about the obligations of the Gentiles to Jewish law. The historical process is seen in how the whole understanding of the sacramental reality within the church developed very slowly, so that for the greater part of its existence the Catholic Church has not acknowledged the existence of seven sacraments. The early church also borrowed concepts of Greek philosophy as it strove to understand better the reality of God and of Jesus Christ. And Thomas Aquinas in the thirteenth century well illustrates creative fidelity in theology by his using Aristotelian philosophy to understand better the mysteries of Christian faith.

In the commitment of the whole church to creative fidelity theologians have an important role to play. One should expect that theologians will be on the cutting edge, pushing, probing, and raising new questions. There would be no development without theological exploration. There will also be theologians who fear that new developments go too far and insist on the need to repudiate some new proposals. History reminds us that theologians will be the first ones to propose new questions, analyses, and syntheses and thereby serve creative fidelity. However, some theologians will go too far and depart from fidelity to the gospel message. Thus history also reminds us of the errors of theologians and the need for the total church to be vigilant.

A Catholic theologian recognizes the role of the theologian in the church and knows that there will be an inescapable tension between the theologian and the pastoral teaching office in the church. Even the greatest and most respected theologians in the church have had their difficulty with church authority. Thomas Aquinas (d. 1274), the patron saint of Catholic theologians and philosophers, was posthumously condemned by some local church authorities. St. Alphonsus Liguori (d. 1787), the patron saint of Catholic moral theologians, was refused clearance by official church censors for his work and was violently attacked by pseudonymous authors who claimed that he was destroying the church. The recent history of the Second Vatican Council shows that the theological leaders of the council — Yves Congar, Henri de Lubac, Marie Dominique Chenu, John Courtney Murray, Teilhard de Chardin, Karl Rahner, and others — all had run-ins with church authority before the council. However, history bears witness that other theologians have gone too far and have not been faithful to the gospel message.

In this light one recognizes the tension that will always exist between theologians and the official teaching office of the church. At times it will not be clear who is right. Thanks to historical hindsight it is easy for us now to know who was right and who was wrong at particular moments in the past. In the future people will be able to look back and see better what is taking place in our times, but in the meantime we ourselves must work through the problems of the present.

The Catholic theologian will always experience this tension. I am under no illusions about the limitations and weaknesses of my own moral theology. I have not produced a totally systematic moral theology but have rather responded to the individual issues and methodological questions as they have arisen in these changing times. I belong to that large group of minor theologians who will make their impact but will probably not make remarkably new breakthroughs or long-standing contributions. Perhaps such is the fate of all moral theologians, but I am certain that it is very true of myself. It is fair to say today that Catholic moral theologians throughout the world and especially here in the United States are feeling the pressures and difficulties of their work. I am not the only one who has been disciplined, even though I may be the most visible one. In a certain sense many of us moral theologians are basically in the same circumstances and working for the same goals as well as experiencing the existing tensions between the role of theologians and the hierarchical teaching office in the church. Tensions will always exist, but these problems today are more exacerbated than they should be.

Self-criticism not only enables me to recognize the limits of my own theological work, but it also reminds me that patience is not a strong suit in my own life. I do not like to wait

in line for anything. I usually find the shortest distance between two points whether I am walking or driving a car. However, in the larger and more significant matters I have been
able, thanks in part to this historical perspective of what has
happened in the church, to be much more patient. I am willing to wait to see through the eyes of history what the final
outcome of the present controversy will be. I remain convinced that I am right, but I do not necessarily need instant
acceptance by the hierarchical church teaching office. I do
not like to see people hurt in the meantime, but for myself
I can await the verdict of history. Thus these three different
ecclesiological perspectives have definitely influenced my desire
to remain a committed Roman Catholic despite the problems
of the present.

Theological Perspectives

One of the reasons bolstering my commitment to the
Roman Catholic community has been its theological tradition. Catholic theology makes sense to me precisely because
it gives great importance to the human and human reason,
and in my judgment this theology justifies the approaches I
have taken.

Karl Barth once maintained that his greatest problem with
Roman Catholicism was its "and." There is no doubt that
Catholicism has stressed the "and" — especially in comparison
with some Protestant theologies. Recall the many ways in
which Catholic thought insists on the "and" — God and the
human, not God alone; grace and nature, not grace alone;
grace and works, not grace alone; scripture and tradition, not
scripture alone; faith and reason, not faith alone; Jesus and
the church and Mary and the saints, not Jesus alone. The
Catholic insistence on the "and" is definitely distinctive. These
distinctive aspects of the Catholic theological tradition are
often mentioned and discussed throughout this volume. I frequently make appeal to one or another of them. However,
it is helpful to consider them together and thereby show what
has been and is characteristic of the Roman Catholic theological tradition.

In my judgment the glory of Catholic theology is its "and," even though there have been mistakes and aberrations along the way. Mistakes have been made in the past through a tendency to absolutize the second element in the couplet and not to see it in relationship to the first element. For example, the danger in Catholicism was to give too much independent importance to tradition and not to see it in relationship to the word of God in scripture. Another error absolutized the church and especially the church as institution instead of seeing it in relationship to and dependent on Jesus and the Spirit. However, in my judgment the Catholic "and" gives due credit to the human and the role of human reason in the light of faith.

Consider first the relationship of God and the human as well as the relationship between grace and nature. An age-old problem for theology concerns the relationship between God and the human. The danger exists of emphasizing God at the expense of the human as well as the opposite danger of emphasizing the human at the expense of God. How do you put the two together? Is it necessary to detract from the human if one wants to emphasize God? Catholic theology employs the principle of participation or mediation to solve this dilemma. It is a false dichotomy to say that one can put the emphasis on God only at the expense of a proper emphasis on the human. According to the Catholic understanding the human person shares and participates in the reality, the truth, and the beauty of God. The glory of God is the human person come alive. The more human we are the closer we resemble God and thereby give glory to God. Glory to God and human fulfillment are not opposed but actually are joined together.

In the moral theology of St. Thomas the human person shares and participates ever more as an image of God precisely insofar as the human person is endowed with intellect, free will, and the power of self-determination. The more free we are the closer we are to God.

The Catholic tradition has also insisted on grace and nature, understood as the human apart from grace. An age-old axiom of Catholic spirituality maintains that grace does not destroy nature but builds on nature. There have been some problems in putting together grace and nature, but the basic thrust of the Catholic approach insists on the goodness of the human. Grace does not destroy the human, but grace brings the human to its greatest possible perfection. In a Thomistic understanding happiness is the end of all human beings and occurs when the basic human drives in the human person — the intellect and the will — attain their end. The end of the intellect is to know the perfect truth, and the end of the will is to love the perfect good. In union with God through grace the human can come to this fulfillment and happiness.

The insistence on grace and works, like the insistence on the human, has often succumbed to the danger of pelagianism, which gives too much importance to human effort. However, properly understood, the need for works is the human response to the divine gift and the human cooperation with it. Thus in the Roman Catholic tradition humanism has never been a pejorative term precisely because this tradition sees grace and God as bringing the human to its perfection. I too have criticized the Catholic tradition and methodology at times for forgetting the presence of sin and not giving enough importance to it, but still its appreciation of the human in all its dimensions remains its characteristic approach. Such an acceptance of and openness to the human is something I appreciate and value in Catholic theology.

The Catholic emphasis on scripture and tradition contrasts with the axiom "the scripture alone." Understood in its best sense the scripture-and-tradition approach grounds the need for creative fidelity which characterizes the church and theology. The word of God must always become incarnate in time and history. The circumstances of first-century Palestine differ from our own circumstances and understandings. It is never enough for the Christian Church or the Christian theologian merely to repeat the words of the scripture. The word of God must be understood, appropriated, and lived in the light of the present historical situation. Such an understanding takes seriously the human and its historical situation. The reality of creative fidelity has been illustrated already within the history of Catholic theology.

The Catholic insistence on faith and reason has at times erred by a reductionism, but at its best this understanding recognizes the role of reason in the epistemological order just as the human is appreciated in the metaphysical order. Yes, faith transcends reason, but faith also uses reason and learns from reason. Medieval theologians staunchly insisted that faith and reason can never contradict one another. This is a magnificent expression of the goodness and importance of human reason. Recall that the medieval theologians themselves were among the first scientists, and the first universities began in medieval times under the auspices of the church. Faith does not have to be fearful of reason. Unfortunately Catholic history is strewn with examples of the failure to live in accord with this bold medieval statement. Too many times the Catholic tradition has lost its nerve and has truly not been open to the truths of human reason.

The Catholic insistence on reason is especially evident in moral theology. The Catholic approach insists that most of its moral teachings are based not on faith alone but on the natural law which through reason is accessible to all human beings. For this reason Catholic moral theology must always be open to dialogue with and learn from philosophy and all the human sciences. For the same reason I remain confident that the Catholic Church must ultimately accept my positions with regard to dissent and the need to change some of its teachings.

The emphasis on Jesus and the church sees the church community as mediating in time and space the word and work of the risen Jesus. However, the danger of such an approach is to absolutize the church when it is only a medium. There can be no doubt that Catholic history has too often succumbed to that temptation. However, other Christians do not give enough importance to the human and insist on an invisible church which sees the Christian related directly and immediately to God. Catholic ecclesiology insists on a visible human community with structures to give it its specific nature whereby this human community mediates God's presence in the world through Jesus and the Spirit. The whole Catholic sacramental system shows forth the role and importance of the human. The basic human reality of eating at a banquet or anointing with water and oil become the signs and symbols of the presence of God's saving grace in our midst.

Within Roman Catholicism the other side of the coin concerns the problem that will always arise from the human element in the church precisely because God has chosen to work in and through the human despite the limitations, imperfections, and even sinfulness which will always characterize the human. Yes, the church is divine, but it is also human and even sinful. In recognizing the sinful element of the church one is also conscious of one's own sinfulness and can never throw the first stone. Such an ecclesiology truly underscores God's willingness to work in and through the human despite all the possible problems.

The Roman Catholic theological tradition in its understanding of faith gives great importance to the human and to human reason. Such an approach makes sense to me and also serves as the basis for my feeling that the church ultimately must change its absolute teaching on the matters involved in my dispute with the Vatican.

In conclusion, I disagree with some noninfallible hierarchical teachings on specific issues. However, it is important for me to put my difficulties with the church in a proper perspective which sees them as only a part of a much larger picture. I remain a committed Roman Catholic because Christian faith mediated through the visible church community is very significant to me personally, and the Catholic theological self-understanding with its acceptance of the human and human reason is very attractive and persuasive. It is precisely in the light of this background that I have made my reaction to Rome a teaching moment in the attempt to bring about change in the church to which I remain committed. However, in the meantime I worry that this church is losing some of its credibility.

4: The Development of Sexual Ethics in Contemporary Roman Catholicism

Sexuality is a very significant aspect of human existence, and all human cultures have tried to discover its meaning and the values and norms that should govern sexuality. Sexual morality and sexual ethics have always been significant issues in the Christian tradition. Within the Roman Catholic Church today sexual questions and ethics have become one of the most vital areas of debate and concern.

The official teaching of the Roman Catholic Church in sexual matters is widely known. But equally well known is that the majority of Catholic believers disagree with the official hierarchical teaching on such issues as the absolute condemnation of masturbation, contraception, sterilization, and divorce. There is also a strong questioning of the teaching on homosexuality and some disagreement on premarital sexuality. This general attitude has been documented in many opinion polls. At the Synod of Bishops in Rome in 1980 Archbishop John R. Quinn cited a Princeton University study showing that 76.5 percent of American Catholic married women of child-bearing age used some form of contraception, and 94 percent of them used a means condemned by the pope.[1]

Many married couples who use artificial contraception have continued to participate in the total life of the church. The same is true for some divorced and remarried Catholics as well as for some gays. From my perspective such reactions

74

can be very good and indicate the legitimacy of practical dissent within the church despite some attempts to prevent it.

However, the present situation of great discrepancy between Catholic teaching and Catholic practice in sexual morality also has significant negative effects. The credibility of the hierarchical teaching office is called into question. As a result of many of these sexual teachings a good number of Roman Catholics have become disillusioned and left the church. Andrew Greeley and his associates on the basis of their sociological findings and analysis have come to the conclusion that *Humanae Vitae*, the 1968 encyclical condemning artificial contraception, "seems to have been the reason for massive apostasy and for a notable decline in religious devotion and belief."[2] Greeley has admitted that he first thought that the deterioration of American Catholic belief and practice would have occurred even without the encyclical, but his research made him change his mind.

On the more theoretical and ethical levels the vast majority of Catholic theologians writing in this area have challenged the basis for the official Catholic teaching. The very nature of official Catholic teaching on sexual ethics occasioned this type of challenge. The Roman Catholic Church and its hierarchical teaching authority have maintained that its teaching is based on the natural law and hence in principle is open to rational acceptance by all human beings. The church does recognize that reason is illumined by faith in these matters, but nonetheless the natural-law methodology claims that the teaching is based on human reason reflecting on human nature and not directly on faith or revelation.

The majority of Catholic ethicists as well as practically all non-Catholic theologians have found the present hierarchical teaching and its theoretical basis to be wanting. The official teaching still rests on the innate purpose and finality of the sexual faculty. The faculty has a twofold purpose — procreation and love union. Every sexual act or actuation must express this twofold finality. This understanding of the sexual faculty and the sexual act forms the basis for the condemnations of masturbation, contraception, sterilization, and homosexual acts. Note that such an understanding also grounds the condemnation of artificial insemination even with the husband's semen (AIH). The next chapter will discuss in greater detail the methodology used in official Catholic sexual teaching.

Many people in the past mistakenly thought that the core of the Roman Catholic position was its pronatalist emphasis. Such is not the case. The ultimate basis of the Catholic teaching is the need for and the inviolability of a sexual act which must be open to procreation and expressive of love. Contraception is wrong because the act is not open to procreation; AIH is wrong because the act of insemination is not the natural act which by its very nature is expressive of love. In this light I have pointed out that the primary problem with the official hierarchical teaching is its physicalism or biologism. The physical act must always be present, and no one can interfere with the physical or biological aspect for any reason whatsoever. The physical becomes absolutized. Most revisionist Catholic theologians today will argue that for the good of the person or for the good of the marriage it is legitimate at times to interfere with the physical structure of the act. Note that it is precisely in questions of sexual morality that Catholic teaching has absolutized the physical and identified the physical with the truly human or moral aspect. For example, there has always existed an important distinction between killing and murder, since murder is the morally condemned act, whereas killing is the physical act which is not always wrong. However, artificial contraception understood as a physical act is said to be always and everywhere wrong.

In the area of sexual ethics church authorities have taken action against some theologians who have dissented on matters of sexual morality. My case is by no means the only example. Stephan Pfürtner in Switzerland, the late Ambrogio Valsecchi in Italy, and Anthony Kosnik in the United States have all lost their teaching positions because of their writings on sexuality. Some Catholic theologians continue to defend the hierarchical teaching of the Catholic Church in sexual matters, but the vast majority of theologians express significant disagreement from this teaching.

This overview and analysis of the sexual teaching and sexual ethics in the contemporary Roman Catholic Church indicates that the primary question or problem in developing a sexual ethic today is not the ethical question itself but the ecclesiological question of dissent and authoritative church teaching. The official hierarchical teaching office of the church appears determined to maintain its present teaching and even to discipline some of the theologians who propose other positions. Anyone interested in changing the official hierarchical sexual teaching and sexual ethics must first deal with the ecclesiological question. Can and should the official hierarchical teaching allow theological and practical dissent in these areas? Can and should the hierarchical office change its teaching in these areas?

I have kidded some of my colleagues in ecclesiology by saying that the real ecclesiological issues today, especially those involving the teaching authority in the church, are being faced by moral theologians particularly in the area of sexual morality and sexual ethics. Why is this the case? Many reasons help to explain this reality. Obviously sexuality is a very significant matter which personally affects everyone. When you put sexuality and authority together, you are bound to have a volatile situation. The official hierarchical teaching in sexual matters has a long history, and this teaching has been inculcated at all levels of education. Thus both history and the very nature of the sexual question show how much the teaching office of the church has been involved in this matter — much more so than in most other areas.

However, a contemporary reason also exists why the area of sexual ethics is so troublesome today and is so entwined with ecclesiological concerns. All must admit that the Second Vatican Council brought about great changes in the theology and life of the Roman Catholic Church. There can and will be debates about the extent and depth of these changes. Today most commentators and theologians recognize the compromise nature of most of the conciliar documents. Newer aspects and approaches are definitely proposed, but often some of the older aspects and approaches are maintained. However, all must admit that the conciliar process itself definitely brought about real change in the life of the church. Many of the documents prepared by the preconciliar commissions were rejected *in toto* by the council. These preliminary documents expressed the neo-Scholastic manualistic theology of the times. Such an approach no longer reigned supreme after the council. In the areas of ecumenism, the church, religious liberty, faith, and revelation very significant developments occurred in and through the conciliar process.

However, sexual morality and sexual ethics went through no such development at Vatican II. The most important issue of the time was that of artificial contraception. But Pope Paul VI took this issue out of the council's hands and reserved it to himself.[3] Finally in 1968 Paul VI issued his encyclical *Humanae Vitae* condemning artificial contraception for married couples as intrinsically evil. It should be noted that Pope Paul VI never issued another encyclical in the remaining years of his pontificate. Sexual morality and sexual ethics, understood as the more systematic, coherent, consistent, theoretical explanation of sexual morality, went through no change or development at Vatican II. Consequently this area of morality is still based on the neo-Scholastic understanding of the manuals of moral theology which were in existence before the Second Vatican Council.

This reality was brought home to me again as a result of some of my reading in March 1987. Herbert Vorgrimler's *Understanding Rahner* gives some biographical information on Rahner based especially on his correspondence. Frequently in the preparatory and early phases of the Second Vatican Council Rahner spoke of the original drafts and the continual struggles against the manualistic theology of the time in these commission meetings. He mentions in this connection on many occasions the theology of Sebastian Tromp and also the work of Franz Hürth.[4] I was somewhat interested because both of these Jesuit theologians had been my professors at the Gregorian University in the 1950s. In fact I would occasionally have long Latin conversations with Hürth, who was always cordial and seemed to enjoy such meetings. In my later years I changed my thinking quite a bit, but I remember with fondness my occasional conversations with Hürth.

At the same time in early March the Congregation for the Doctrine of the Faith issued its "Instruction on Respect for

Human Life in Its Origin and on the Dignity of Procreation." The issue that drew the most disagreement within the Roman Catholic community was the rejection of *in vitro* fertilization using the husband's seed on the grounds that artificial insemination even with the husband's seed was always morally wrong. The footnotes to the condemnation of homologous artificial insemination (AIH) referred to Pope Pius XII's "Discourse to Those Taking Part in the Fourth International Congress of Catholic Doctors, September 29, 1949."[5] In this address the pope condemned AIH as violating the divine plan because the natural conjugal act itself was not present.

There are two interesting comments that must be made about the 1949 papal address. First, before the address a number of Catholic moralists held that in practice artificial insemination between husband and wife could be permitted provided the husband's sperm was obtained in some legitimate way. This condition referred to the fact that those authors thought masturbation was intrinsically evil and could never be the means of obtaining the semen. Even as conservative a Catholic moral theologian as Thomas J. O'Donnell admits that AIH was an open question in theory and in practice before 1949.[6] Thus it is hard to speak about a traditional teaching of the Roman Catholic Church in this regard.

A second note about this document is most fascinating. A commentary on the September 29 papal address written by Franz Hürth appeared in the September 15, 1949, issue of *Periodica*.[7] It was well known that Hürth wrote most of Pius XII's addresses on moral issues. One Roman wag commented that in this case they had to hold back the publication of the commentary until the address itself was given!

It the light of the Rahner history and the new document of the Congregation for the Doctrine of the Faith I became existentially very aware that Catholic moral teaching in 1987 was still based on the neo-Scholasticism of the pre-Vatican II manuals of moral theology. If this same reality were true in other areas such as revelation, the church, ecumenism, and religious liberty, the Roman Catholic Church would look quite different today.

What would have happened if Vatican II had discussed

and decided the issue of artificial contraception? Perhaps the teaching would have been changed especially in the light of the other changes which occurred at that time. Undoubtedly the major issue would have been how can the church now accept something which it had earlier condemned. How could there be such a change or development in the official teaching of the church? The best illustration of change at Vatican II was the teaching on religious freedom. Here John Courtney Murray and others proposed a theory of development based on changing historical circumstances. In the nineteenth century the church rightly condemned the understanding of religious freedom based on Continental liberalism, but in the twentieth century religious liberty, understood as a civil right of immunity in a limited constitutional government structure, could be accepted.[8] This theory of development downplayed the discontinuity factor and employed the changing historical circumstances to justify the change. It is easy in retrospect to criticize this theory for failing to recognize that somewhere along the line the teaching of the church was wrong or should have been changed sooner. In the area of contraception it probably would have been necessary to face head-on the issue of the existence of error in the official teaching of the hierarchical magisterium.

It is impossible for anyone to know what would have happened if Vatican II had debated the questions of artificial contraception and of sexual morality. Two things are certain today. First, in the area of sexual morality and ethics there has been no development within the church's teaching as there has been in many other areas debated at Vatican II. How often in other areas of teaching in theology would a 1949 papal address on a specific issue be totally normative? Second, the primary issue today in the hierarchical Catholic sexual teaching remains the issue of change in the teaching and the ecclesial question of the nature of the hierarchical teaching office.

Many reasons help to explain the reluctance on the part of people in authority to change the official church teaching in this matter or to allow the possibility of dissent. The patriarchal nature of the church and of its teaching on human sexuality cannot be denied. The Catholic Church has excluded women from any kind of significant decision-making role in the life of the church. I am sure that the desire for control of others and a celibate fear of sexuality have also contributed to the present hierarchical teaching and to the reluctance to change it. However, those of us working for such changes must address the most significant issues raised by the defenders of the present teaching even though we recognize there are other factors that also support this teaching.

The strongest reason for maintaining the present teaching in the eyes of its defenders is one's understanding of the teaching function of the church. The hierarchical teaching function of the church is believed to be under the power and guidance of the Holy Spirit. Could the Holy Spirit ever permit the hierarchical teaching office to be wrong in a matter of such great import in the lives of so many Christian people? The church and the officially commissioned leaders of the church have their role as mediating the salvific word and work of Jesus through the presence of the Spirit. Could the hierarchical teaching role actually hinder and hurt the people it was supposed to help?

Such questions cannot be easily dismissed. One must at least feel the force of such questions for those who are posing them. The only adequate response to these questions is the recognition that the hierarchical teaching office itself has failed to recognize and teach the proper nature and binding force of such teaching as well as the assent due to such teaching. By its very nature this teaching on these specific and complex questions of the norms governing sexuality involves what has recently been called the authoritative noninfallible hierarchical teaching office. Such teaching according to a 1967 document of the West German bishops has a certain degree of binding force, and yet, since it is not a *de fide* definition, it involves a certain element of the provisional even to the point of being capable of including error.[9]

The ultimate epistemological reason why this teaching cannot claim an absolute certitude comes from the very nature of moral truth. Thomas Aquinas pointed out the difference between speculative and practical or moral truth. In the area of morality with its complexities and many circumstances the secondary principles of the natural law generally oblige but in some cases they do not hold. Thomas uses as an example the natural-law principle that deposits should be returned. An obligation exists to return to the owner what has been given one to care for and keep safe. Such a principle usually obliges but not always. If someone has left you a sword for safekeeping and now wants it back but is drunk and threatening to kill people, you have an obligation not to return the sword.[10] In their two pastoral letters on peace and the economy the United States bishops have recognized the same reality. On the level of complex and specific judgments one cannot claim a certitude that excludes the possibility of error. Thus, for example, the bishops maintain that the first use of counter-force nuclear weapons is always wrong, but they recognize that others within the church community might come to a different conclusion.[11]

Within the traditional understanding of the teaching function of the hierarchical magisterium it is possible for authoritative noninfallible hierarchical teaching on specific moral issues to be wrong. Church authority has added to the existing problem by its failure to recognize explicitly the somewhat provisional nature of its teaching in these areas. In this light one can understand the charge of creeping infallibilism that has been made. Noninfallible teaching is thought to be as certain and absolute as infallible teaching. If the very nature and limitation of such authoritative noninfallible teaching were better understood, the fact of erroneous church teaching would not be as great a problem as one might think. In addition, such a recognition could serve as a very good way of indicating the role of all the baptized contributing in different ways to the teaching of the church and also be a salutary reminder that the hierarchical teaching authority has not carried out its own learning and teaching function in the most suitable way.

For any of us to admit we have made mistakes is very difficult. It is obviously very difficult for the hierarchical teaching office with its understanding of having the assistance of the Holy Spirit to recognize that its teachings might be wrong. However, history does record the existence of such errors in the past, and Catholic self-understanding acknowledges the theoretical possibility of such errors. A recognition of mistakes by church authority would not be unprecedented. The Decree on Ecumenism (n. 7) of Vatican Council II humbly recognizes there has been sin on all sides in the work for church unity and begs pardon of God and our separated brothers and sisters just as we forgive those who have trespassed against us. In the present situation the first step that can and should be made is the official recognition of the somewhat provisional character of the authoritative noninfallible hierarchical teaching in these areas. From this there follows the possibility and perhaps at times even the legitimacy of dissent both in theory and in practice.

What about the credibility of the hierarchical teaching office if it explicitly recognizes the legitimacy of dissent or even changes its teaching? How can anyone ever again put trust and confidence in such a teaching office? It must be pointed out that there already exists a very great problem of credibility for the hierarchical teaching office in sexual matters. When the vast majority of the members of the church disagree with the official hierarchical teaching on issues such as contraception, there truly exists a problem of confidence in that authority. The case can be made that the hierarchical teaching office would gain credibility if it recognizes the possibility of dissent and even changes its teaching in this area.

In my view dissent from the authoritative noninfallible hierarchical teaching of the Roman Catholic Church tries to support and not destroy the credibility of this teaching office. The hierarchical teaching office in general would be more credible if it is clear to all that the critical interpretative function of Catholic theologians at times might call for dissent from the teaching of the hierarchical magisterium. Here the theological community can play the critical role of the loyal opposition and thus enhance in the long run the hierarchical teaching role in the church.

To carry out its teaching role properly the hierarchical magisterium must be in dialogue with the whole church. The primary teacher in the church remains the Holy Spirit, and no one has a monopoly on the Holy Spirit. Wide consultation and dialogue are a necessary part of the function of the hierarchical teaching office. Unfortunately such dialogue and consultation have not occurred in the area of sexual morality, and the credibility of the hierarchical teaching office has suffered.

Compare, for example, the process involved in writing the pastoral letters of the United States bishops and the process involved in writing the recent Roman documents such as the instruction of the Congregation for the Doctrine of the Faith on bioethics. The American bishops engaged in a broad consultation process and shared their drafts with the whole world in a very public dialogue. Also the bishops recognized different levels of teaching and the different responses due to the various levels. The pastoral letters distinguish the levels of principle and universal teaching on the one hand from that of specific judgments and conclusions. Legitimate diversity can exist within the church in the realm of specific judgments and even complex specific norms. I agree very much with this basic approach, which recognizes that the possibility of certitude decreases as the matter under consideration becomes more specific and complex. However, even here there is a tendency in the pastoral letters to claim too much agreement and certitude on the level of principle. The pastoral letter on peace maintains that the independent principle of discrimination or noncombatant immunity is something that must be held by all people within the church. However, the West German bishops in their pastoral letter on war do not accept this independent principle as an absolute norm. Chapter eight will discuss in greater detail the West German and United States pastoral letters on peace. However, the process involved in the writing of the United States pastoral letters has enhanced their credibility. Documents emanating from Rome would have a greater credibility if such a process and approach were employed.

A final objection asks where all this is going to end. Perhaps dissent on one or another issue might be acceptable but not across such a broad spectrum. Is everything up for grabs? Are there no limits?

It is incumbent on those of us within the Roman Catholic

Church who call for a broader area of dissent to address this question and to talk about limits. One must recognize that dissent or, more positively, pluralism exists within a broader area of unity, assent, and agreement. In the Christian faith community not everything is up for grabs. The church is called to creative fidelity with regard to the word and work of Jesus. It is important to recognize the distinction between what is core and central to the faith and what is more remote and peripheral. Today the emphasis on praxis in contemporary theology reminds us that morality and what we do are integral parts of our faith community and our faith commitment. However, specific issues and concrete norms in complex cases require room for more diversity and disagreement. The church must always teach and live the values of love and fidelity in marriage, but it does not follow that divorce and remarriage are wrong in all circumstances. Doubtless there will be greater areas of dissent and pluralism than there were in the past. Also there will be more grey areas than ever before. The methodological understanding of contemporary theology points in this direction. However, these realities of greater pluralism and greater dissent on specific issues still exist side by side with the unity of the church and with a credible hierarchical teaching office in the church. In fact, one could make the case that at the present time such dissent and unity are already existing in practice in the Roman Catholic Church.

There is much disagreement within the Roman Catholic Church today about sexual morality. Church authorities are taking disciplinary action against some theologians writing in these areas and thus preventing the development of a contemporary sexual ethic within Roman Catholicism. There are significant practical and theoretical factors calling for a different understanding of sexual morality and of sexual ethics. However, the biggest obstacle to such developments comes from the practical ecclesiological issue of the hierarchical teaching office. We who are calling for a changed theory and practice of sexuality in the Roman Catholic Church will be successful only if we can convince the church of the need to change some of its current ecclesiological understandings of the hierarchical teaching office and to admit the possibility of dissent and error in such teachings.

NOTES

1. Archbishop John R. Quinn, "New Context for Contraception Teaching," *Origins* 10 (1980): 263-267.

2. Andrew M. Greeley, William C. McCready, and Kathleen McCort, *Catholic Schools in a Declining Church* (Kansas City, MO: Sheed and Ward, 1976), p. 153.

3. Robert Blair Kaiser, *The Politics of Sex and Religion* (Kansas City, MO: Sheed and Ward, 1985), p. 63.

4. Herbert Vorgrimler, *Understanding Karl Rahner: An Introduction to His Life and Thought* (New York: Crossroad, 1986), pp. 35, 52, 94, 96, 136, 156, 157, 162, 166, 168ff.

5. Congregation for the Doctrine of the Faith, "Instruction on Respect for Human Life in Its Origin and on the Dignity of Procreation," *Origins* 16 (1987): 697ff., II, B, 5.

6. Thomas J. O'Donnell, *Medicine and Christian Morality* (New York: Alba House, 1976), p. 266.

7. Franciscus Hürth, "Annotationes," *Periodica de re Morali, Canonica, Liturgica* 38 (1949): 282-295.

8. John Courtney Murray, *The Problem of Religious Freedom* (Westminster, MD: Newman Press, 1965), pp. 47-84.

9. This document is cited at great length by Karl Rahner, *Theological Investigations*, vol. XIV: *Ecclesiology, Questions in the Church, the Church in the World* (New York: Seabury Press, 1976), p. 86.

10. Thomas Aquinas, *Summa Theologiae, Pars Ia IIae* (Rome: Marietti, 1952), q.94, a.4.

11. For a more in-depth discussion of dissent representing the most significant positions see Charles E. Curran and Richard A. McCormick, eds., *Readings in Moral Theology No. 3: The Magisterium and Morality* (New York: Paulist Press, 1982).

5: Official Catholic Social and Sexual Teachings: A Methodological Comparison

The official hierarchical teaching of the Roman Catholic Church in moral matters has importance not only for the church members themselves but also for others in society at large. The attention given to this moral teaching in the popular press illustrates the news worthiness attached to it. Thanks to the popular media people in the United States were widely alerted to the stance taken by the United States Roman Catholic bishops on war and the economy as well as the position of the Vatican on test-tube babies.

A general impression is in evidence both within and outside the Catholic Church that Catholic moral teaching in social and sexual areas appears to be somewhat different. From the perspective of the general public contemporary Catholic social teaching with its criticism of the United States economic system and of our nuclear war and deterrence policy falls into what is often called the "liberal camp." However, Catholic teaching in sexual matters is definitely in the more "conservative camp."

The impression of differences between official Catholic social and sexual teaching also exists within the Catholic Church itself. Many conservative and neoconservative Roman Catholics have objected strenuously to the recent social teachings of the United States bishops but seem to have no problems with the official church teaching on sexual ethics. On the other hand, liberal Catholics have applauded the recent social teachings while often dissenting from the sexual teachings.

The purpose of this chapter is not to discuss the relationship between social and sexual ethics; nor will I take sides in the dispute between "liberal" and "conservative" Catholics, even though my own position is well known. My purpose is to examine the ethical methodology employed in each of these two aspects of official Catholic moral teachings and to point out the clear differences between the methodologies.

Catholic Social Teaching

Today a body of official Catholic social teaching exists going back to Pope Leo XIII's encyclical *Rerum Novarum* in 1891.[1] Subsequent encyclicals and official documents were often issued on anniversaries of *Rerum Novarum*, such as Pope Pius XI's *Quadragesimo Anno*[2] in 1931, Pope John XXIII's *Mater et Magistra*[3] in 1961, Pope Paul VI's *Octogesima Adveniens*[4] in 1971, and Pope John Paul II's *Laborem Exercens*[5] in 1981. In addition there are other papal documents as well as documents from the Second Vatican Council and the synods of bishops which constitute this body of official Catholic social teaching.

One significant question about these documents and other hierarchical social teaching concerns the authoritative nature of such teaching and the response which is due to such teaching on the part of Roman Catholic believers. To discuss the nature, extent, and limits of authoritative teaching in the Catholic Church lies beyond the scope of the present considerations. However, one point should be made. There are many other hierarchical church teachings from Pope Leo XIII and later which are no longer remembered today. Leo's teaching on the political order is seldom read or even mentioned on the contemporary scene. Leo's political writings generally insist on at best a paternalistic or at worst an authoritarian view of society.[6] The unofficial canon of Catholic social teaching today has been brought about by the reception of the church itself—the voices of subsequent popes but also the response of the total church. The whole church has played a role in what is viewed today as constituting the body of official Catholic social teaching.

Within the documents themselves the popes and the episcopal bodies explicitly stress the continuity with what went before. Popes are very fond of quoting their predecessors of happy memory. However, in reality much change and development have occurred within this body of social teaching. This section will study three important methodological issues which have experienced a very significant change in the less than 100-year historical span covered by this body of official Catholic social teaching. These methodological changes in social teaching will be contrasted in the following section with the official teaching on sexual ethics which has not experienced such changes. The three methodological areas to be considered are the shift to historical consciousness, the shift to personalism, and the acceptance of a relationality-responsibility ethical model. Each of these methodological developments will now be traced.

Shift to Historical Consciousness[7]

Historical consciousness is often contrasted with classicism. Classicism understands reality in terms of the eternal, the immutable, and the unchanging; whereas historical consciousness gives more importance to the particular, the contingent, the historical, and the individual. Historical consciousness should also be contrasted with the other extreme of sheer existentialism. Sheer existentialism sees the present moment in isolation from the before and the after of time, with no binding relationships to persons and values in the present. Historical consciousness recognizes the need for both continuity and discontinuity. This discussion about worldview tends to be primarily a philosophical endeavor, but there are relationships to the theological. The Catholic theological tradition has recognized historicity in its rejection of the axiom "the scripture alone." The scripture must always be understood, appropriated, communicated, and lived in the light of the historical and cultural realities of the present time. The church just cannot repeat the words of the scriptures. Catholicism has undergone much more development than most people think. While creative fidelity is necessary for any tradition, such creative fidelity is consistent with the philosophical world-view of historical consciousness.

These two different worldviews spawn two different meth-odological approaches. The classicist worldview is associated with the deductive methodology that deduces its conclusions from its premises, which are eternal verities. The syllogism well illustrates the deductive approach. Note that in such an approach one's conclusions are as certain as the premises if the logic is correct. Historical consciousness recognizes the need for a more inductive approach. However, the need to maintain both continuity as well as discontinuity argues against a one-sided inductive approach. An inductive approach by its very nature can never achieve the same degree of certi-tude for its conclusions as does the deductive methodology of the classicist worldview.

There can be no doubt that a significant development toward historical consciousness has occurred in the body of official social teaching. Pope Pius XI's 1931 encyclical *Quadra-gesimo Anno* is often called in English "On Reconstructing the Social Order."[8] In this encyclical the pope proposes his plan for this reorganization, which is often called moderate cor-poratism or solidarism. In keeping with the traditional em-phasis in the Catholic tradition this papal plan sees all the dif-ferent institutions that are part of society as working together for the common good of all. Catholic social teaching has in-sisted on the metaphor of society as an organism with all the parts existing for the good of the totality. According to such an outlook labor and capital should not be adversaries fighting one another, but rather they should work together for the com-mon good. Moderate corporatism sees labor, capital, and con-sumers all working together and forming one group to con-trol what happens in a particular industry. This group would set prices, wages, and the amount of goods to be produced. Then other such groups on a higher level would coordinate and direct the individual industries and professions.

Pope Pius XI proposed his plan for reconstruction as some-thing applicable to the whole world. Of course, the world of Pius XI and his contemporaries was primarily the Euro-centric world. The deductive nature of the plan is quite evident in the encyclical. From a philosophical view of society as an organism the pope sketched out his approach as a middle course between the extremes of individualistic capitalism and collective socialism. In reality this plan had little chance of succeeding precisely because it did not correspond to any existing historical reality, and the popes never entered into the debate of making the plan work in practice. Pope Pius XII, the successor of Pope Pius XI, spoke less and less about this plan as his pontificate continued, and Pope John XXIII basically ignored the proposal.[9]

Such a deductive methodology is in keeping with the neo-Scholastic thesis-approach to theology. However, some developments gradually occurred. Pope John XXIII's 1963 encyclical *Pacem in Terris* still follows a generally deductive approach, but in this and in his earlier encyclical *Mater et Magistra* Pope John XXIII did not give attention to the plan for reconstruction proposed by Pope Pius XI. However, at the end of each of the four chapters or parts of *Pacem in Terris* there is a short section on the signs of the times—the special characteristics of the present day.[10] Two years later *Gaudium et Spes*, the Pastoral Constitution of the Church in the Modern World of the Second Vatican Council, gives a much greater emphasis to historical consciousness. Each of the five chapters in the second part of the document deals with a specific area of concern and each begins with the signs of the times.

Pope Paul VI's Apostolic Letter *Octogesima Adveniens* of 1971 shows a very heightened awareness of historical consciousness:

> In the face of such widely varying situations it is difficult for us to utter a unified message and to put forward a solution which has universal validity. Such is not our ambition, nor is it our mission. It is up to the Christian communities to analyze with objectivity the situation which is proper to their own country, to shed on it the light of the Gospel's unalterable words and to draw principles of reflection, norms of judgment, and directives for action from the social teaching of the church. . . . It is up to these Christian communities, with the help of the Holy Spirit, in communion with the bishops who hold responsibility and in dialogue with other Christian brethren and all people of good

will, to discern the options and commitments which are called
for in order to bring about the social, political, and economic
changes seen in many cases to be urgently needed.[11]

Only forty years earlier Pope Pius XI had put forward a plan
for social reconstruction which in his mind had universal validity. The difference between the approaches of thse two popes
is very great.

The more inductive methodology of *Octogesima Adveniens*
gives great importance to contemporary developments. A large
portion of the letter is devoted to two aspirations that have
come to the fore in the contemporary consciousness:

> While scientific and technological progress continues to overturn
> human surroundings, patterns of knowledge, work, consump-
> tion, and relationships, two aspirations persistently make them-
> selves felt in these new contexts, and they grow stronger to the
> extent that one becomes better informed and better educated:
> the aspiration to equality and the aspiration to participation,
> two forms of human dignity and freedom.[12]

It must be pointed out that the present pope, John Paul II,
has pulled back somewhat from Pope Paul VI's insistence on
historical consciousness. *Laborem Exercens*, the 1981 encyclical,
is a philosophical reflection on work and its meaning that is
intended to address all people. In his other writings John
Paul II definitely moves away from the historical consciousness of Paul VI. His Christology, for example, is a Christology
from above which begins with the eternally begotten Word
of God and not with the historical Jesus.

Two reasons help to explain John Paul II's reluctance to
embrace historical consciousness as much as his predecessor
did. By temperament and training the present pope is a philos-
opher who studied, taught, and wrote in the more classical
philosophical mode. Such thinking and writing are clearly con-
genial to him. In addition, historical consciousness can be
seen as somewhat of a threat to the unity and central authority
in the church. All today recognize the tensions existing between the church universal as represented by the bishop of
Rome and the national and local churches. Local diversity

and pluralism are seen as threats to the unity and authority of the church. There can be no doubt that these existing tensions have made Pope John Paul II very wary of historical consciousness.

However, the present pope does not use a more classicist approach to avoid making some very concrete and critical statements about existing social reality. *Laborem Exercens* does not shrink from criticizing many aspects of the plight of the worker today.

Recent Catholic social theology and ethics have embraced the concept of historical consciousness. Consider, for example, the whole field of liberation theology as well as the importance given to praxis and to social analysis in recent writings.

Shift to the Person with an Emphasis on Freedom, Equality, and Participation

Within the time frame of a one-hundred-year span there has been a very significant shift in Catholic social teaching away from an emphasis on human nature with a concomitant stress on order, the acceptance of some inequality, and away from obedience to the many controlling authorities to a recognition of the vital importance of the human person with the concomitant need for human freedom, equality, and participation.

In the nineteenth century the Catholic Church opposed freedom and the thought of the Enlightenment. Freedom in religion, philosophy, science, and politics threatened the old order in all its aspects. Individualistic freedom forgot about human beings' relationships to God, to God's law, to human society in general, and to other human beings. Continental liberalism with its emphasis on the individualistic freedom was seen as the primary enemy of the church.[13] Even in the nineteenth century official Catholic teaching did not condemn all slavery as always wrong.[14]

Pope Leo XIII was very much a part of this tradition. He stressed order and social cohesiveness rather than freedom. God's law and the natural law govern human existence. Leo's view of society was authoritarian or at least paternalistic. He often referred to the people as the ignorant multitude that had to be led by their rulers. (Such an approach is somewhat understandable in the light of the low state of European literacy at the time.) In social ethics freedom was seen as a threat to the social organism. Individualistic capitalism was condemned as a form of economic liberalism which claimed that one could pay whatever wage one could get away with. Leo was also no friend of democracy because no majority could do away with God's law, and freedom of religion could never be promoted but at best only tolerated as the lesser evil in certain circumstances.[15]

Development occurred in the methodology of official Catholic social teaching precisely because of changing historical circumstances. The Catholic Church's enemy, or in more recent terminology, the dialogue partner, changed. In the nineteenth century the church opposed the individualistic liberalism of the day. As the twentieth century advanced, the central problem became the rise and existence of totalitarian governments. In this context the Catholic Church began to defend the freedom and dignity of the human person against the encroachments of totalitarianism. Pope Pius XI in the 1930s wrote encyclical letters against fascism, nazism, and communism.[16] In theory the Roman Catholic Church opposed all forms of totalitarianism, but there can be no doubt that the church was more willing in practice to tolerate totalitarianism from the right. After the Second World War Catholic teaching consistently and constantly attacked communism. (Note that in the 1960s a change occurred with Pope John XXIII, and there ensued a much more nuanced dialogical approach to Marxism.)[17] In the light of this polemic Catholic teaching stressed the freedom and dignity of the individual.

Pope John XXIII's *Pacem in Terris* in 1963 signals the Catholic acceptance of the role of freedom. In *Mater et Magistra* in 1961 John XXIII, in keeping with the Catholic tradition, insisted in a major part of this document that the ideal social order rests on the three values of truth, justice and love.[18] Two years later in *Pacem in Terris* the pope adds a fourth element — truth, justice, charity, and freedom.[19] *Pacem in Terris* develops for the first time a full-blown treatment of human rights in the Catholic tradition.[20] Before that time Catholic thought had been fearful of rights language precisely because of the danger of excessive individualism. Catholic social teaching had insisted on duties and obedience to the divine and natural law and not on rights. In its quite late embracing of the human rights tradition *Pacem in Terris* still recognizes the danger of individualism by including economic rights and by insisting on the correlation between rights and duties.

There was one major obstacle or inconsistency in Catholic social teaching in the early 1960s. While the tradition was now insisting on the importance of freedom and the dignity of the individual, official hierarchical teaching still could not accept religious freedom. One of the great accomplishments of the Second Vatican Council in 1965 was the acceptance of religious freedom as demanded by the very dignity of the human person. Religious freedom is understood as freedom from external coercion that forces one to act against one's conscience or prevents one's acting in accord with one's conscience in religious matters.[21] In accepting this teaching Vatican II had to admit that a significant development and even change had occurred in Catholic thinking because in the nineteenth and twentieth century before 1965 official Catholic teaching could not accept religious freedom.[22] In the light of present circumstances one appreciates all the more both the theoretical and the practical import of this change in Catholic teaching.

In 1971 Pope Paul VI in *Octogesima Adveniens* devoted a long section of the document to two new aspirations which have become more persistent and stronger in the contemporary context — the aspiration to equality and the aspiration to participation — two forms of human dignity and freedom.[23]

Pope John Paul II has strengthened and even developed the shift to personalism. *Laborem Exercens* in 1981 emphasizes that the subjective aspect of work is more important than the objective precisely because of the dignity of the human person. The personal aspect of labor is the basis for the priority of labor over capital.

Thus in the twentieth century a very significant shift has occurred in the methodology of Catholic social teaching through its emphasis on the importance of the dignity and freedom of the human person. Catholic personalism is the basis for many changes in particular teachings in the area of social, political, and economic morality.

Shift to a Relationality-Responsibility Ethical Model

In general there are three generic ethical models that have been used to understand the moral life in a more systematic way. The deontological model understands morality primarily in terms of law and obedience to the law. Deontological approaches are often castigated for being legalistic in a pejorative sense, but such is not necessarily the case. (Think, for example, of the legal model developed by Kant with its categorical imperative.) The teleological model understands morality in the light of the end or the goal and the means to attain it. One first determines what is the end or the goal. Something is good if it leads toward that goal and evil if it impedes attaining the goal. In the complexity of human existence there are many various types of goals and ends — the ultimate end, less ultimate ends, subordinate ends, etc. The relationality-responsibility model sees the human person in terms of one's multiple relationships with God, neighbor, world, and self and the call to live responsibly in the midst of these relationships. In systematic understandings of moral theory one of the models will be primary. One word of caution is necessary. Although one of these models is primary, they should not be seen as mutually exclusive. Thus, for example, in a teleological model or in a relationality-responsibility model there will always be place for some laws and norms, but the law model will not be primary.

All agree that the manuals of Catholic moral theology which existed until the time of the Second Vatican Council employed the legal model as primary. According to the manuals of moral theology the proximate, subjective, and intrinsic norm of moral action is conscience. Conscience is the dictate of moral reason about the morality of an act. The remote, objective, and extrinsic norm of moral action is law. The function of conscience is thus to obey the law. Law is either divine law or human law. Divine law is twofold. First, the laws which necessarily follow from God as the author and creator of nature involve the eternal law, which is the order or plan existing in the mind of God, and the natural law, which is the participation of the eternal law in the rational creature. Second, divine positive law comes from the free determination of God as the author of revelation. Human law has human beings as its author and can be either church or civil law. Note that all law shares in the eternal law of God and that human law must always be seen in relationship to and subordinate to the natural law and the eternal law. Thus the manuals of moral theology view the moral life as conscience obeying the various laws.[24] More specifically, Catholic moral teaching has insisted that most of its moral teaching is based on the natural law, which in principle is knowable by all human beings since it is human reason reflecting on human nature.

The emphasis on the legal model as primary in Catholic moral theology before the Second Vatican Council is somewhat anomalous in light of the Catholic tradition. Thomas Aquinas (d. 1274) remains the most significant figure in the Roman Catholic theological tradition. However, Thomas Aquinas in his moral theory was not a deontologist but a teleologist.[25] It is true that Thomas does have a treatise on law and the different types of law just as is found in the manuals, but this treatise on law is comparatively small and appears only at the end of his discussion of ethical theory. Aquinas was an intrinsic teleologist. His first ethical consideration is the ultimate end of human beings. The ultimate end of human beings is happiness, which is achieved when the fundamental powers or drives of human nature achieve their end. The intellect and the will are the most basic human powers. To know the truth and to love the good constitute the basic fulfillment and happiness of the human being. This happiness occurs in the beatific vision. Morality in this view is intrinsic. Something is commanded because it is good for the individual and leads to the ultimate fulfillment and happiness of the individual. However, the neo-Scholasticism of the manuals of moral theology truncated Aquinas' moral thought and reduced it to a deontological model.

There can be no doubt that the Catholic social teaching in the nineteenth and early twentieth centuries basically worked out of a legal model. Even as late as 1963 *Pacem in Terris* recognized the law model to be the primary structural approach of the whole encyclical. *Pacem in Terris* begins by insisting that peace on earth can firmly be established only if the order laid down by God be dutifully observed. An astounding order reigns in our world, and the greatness of human beings is to understand that order. The creator of the world has imprinted on the human heart an order which conscience reveals and enjoins one to obey.[26]

> But fickleness of opinion often produces this error, that many think that the relationships between human beings and states can be governed by the same laws as the forces and irrational elements of the universe, whereas the laws governing them are of quite a different kind and are to be sought elsewhere, namely, where the Father of all things wrote them, that is, in human nature.
>
> By these laws human beings are most admirably taught first of all how they should conduct their mutual dealings among themselves, then how the relationships between the citizens and the public authority of each state should be regulated, then how states should deal with one another, and finally how, on the one hand, individual human beings and states, and, on the other hand, the community of all peoples, should act toward each other, the establishment of such a community being urgently demanded today by the requirements of universal common good.[27]

This introductory section sets the stage for the four parts of the encyclical which are the four areas mentioned above. Thus, the law model is highlighted as the approach still followed in *Pacem in Terris*.

Pope Paul VI's *Octogesima Adveniens* in 1971 well illustrates the shift from a legal model to a relationality-responsibility model. As noted above, Paul VI here strongly endorses a shift to historical consciousness. In such a perspective this document does not look for the order and laws inscribed in human nature. Here the historical character and the dynamism of the church's social teaching are stressed:

It is with all its dynamism that the social teaching of the church accompanies human beings in their search. If it does not intervene to authenticate a given structure or to propose a ready-made model, it does not thereby limit itself to recalling general principles. It develops through reflection applied to the changing situations of this world, under the driving force of the gospel as the source of renewal when its message is accepted in its totality and with all its demands. It also develops with a sensitivity proper to the church which is characterized by a disinterested will to serve and by attention to the poorest. Finally, it draws upon its rich experience of many centuries which enables it, while continuing its permanent preoccupations, to undertake the daring and creative innovations which the present state of the world requires.[28]

Octogesima Adveniens does not see conscience in the light of obedience to law. Chapter nine below will examine in greater detail the understanding of conscience in church documents on social questions. The most characteristic word to describe the function of conscience in this papal letter is discernment (n. 36). Pope Paul VI also introduces into Catholic social teaching the methodological importance of utopias:

The appeal to a utopia is often a convenient excuse for those who wish to escape from concrete tasks in order to take refuge in an imaginary world. To live in a hypothetical future is a facile alibi for rejecting immediate responsibilities. But it must clearly be recognized that this kind of criticism of existing society often provokes the forward-looking imagination both to perceive in the present the discarded possibility hidden within it, and to direct itself toward a fresh future; it thus sustains social dynamism by the confidence that it gives to the inventive powers of the human mind and heart; and, if it refuses no overture, it can also meet the Christian appeal. The Spirit of the Lord, who animates human beings renewed in Christ, continually breaks down the horizons within which one's understanding likes to find security and the limits to which one's activity would willingly restrict itself; there dwells within one a power which urges one to go beyond every system and every ideology. At the heart of the world there dwells the mystery of the human person discovering oneself to be God's child in the course of a historical and psychological process in which constraint and freedom as well as the weight of sin and the breath of the Spirit alternate and struggle for the upper hand.[29]

Octogesima Adveniens ends with a recognition of shared responsibility, a call to action, and the realization of a pluralism of possible options.[30] Thus the letter definitely marks a decided shift toward the primacy of the relationality-responsibility model in Catholic social teaching. Development within official Catholic social teaching has thus occurred on three very important methodological concerns.

Catholic Sexual Teaching

The focus now shifts to official Catholic teaching in the area of sexual morality. Three recent documents will be examined — the "Declaration on Sexual Ethics" issued by the Congregation for the Doctrine of the Faith on December 29, 1975;[31] the "Letter to the Bishops of the Catholic Church on the Pastoral Care of Homosexual Persons" promulgated by the Congregation for the Doctrine of the Faith on October 1, 1986;[32] the "Instruction on Respect for Human Life in Its Origin and on the Dignity of Procreation" issued by the Congregation for the Doctrine of the Faith on February 22, 1987.[33] The present discussion centers on methodological issues, but something must be said briefly about the authoritative nature of these documents. There is a hierarchy of official Catholic Church documents. These three documents are not from the pope himself but from one of the Roman congregations. By their very nature such documents are not expected to break new ground. However, it is interesting that the documents have received wide public discussion. Catholics owe a religious respect to the teaching of these documents, but they are of less authoritative weight than the documents issued by the pope himself.

For our present purposes the focus is on the methodological approaches taken in these documents. This study will show that these methodological approaches differ sharply from the three methodological approaches found in the contemporary documents on Catholic social teaching. Each of these three methodological issues will be considered in turn.

Classicist Rather Than Historically Conscious

The "Declaration on Sexual Ethics" of 1975 shows very little historical consciousness. In the very beginning of the document the emphasis on the eternal and the immutable is very clear:

> Therefore there can be no true promotion of human dignity unless the essential order of human nature is respected. Of course, in the history of civilization many of the concrete conditions and needs of human life have changed and will continue to change. But all evolution of morals and every type of life must be kept within the limits imposed by the immutable principles based upon every human person's constitutive elements and essential relations — elements and relations which transcend historical contingencies.
>
> These fundamental principles which can be grasped by reason are contained in "the divine law — eternal, objective, and universal — whereby God orders, directs, and governs the entire universe and all the ways of human community by a plan conceived in wisdom and love. Human beings have been made by God to participate in this law with the result that under the gentle disposition of divine providence they can come to perceive ever increasingly the unchanging truth." This divine law is accessible to our minds. (n. 3)

The "Letter to the Bishops of the Catholic Church on the Pastoral Care of Homosexual Persons" in 1986 bases its teaching on "the divine plan" and "the theology of creation" which tells us of "the creator's sexual design" (nn. 1-7). The "theocratic law" (n. 6) found in the scripture also attests to the church's teaching. Emphasis is frequently put on the will of God which is known in the above-mentioned ways and is what the church teaches.

This letter points out that many call for a change in the

church's teaching on homosexuality because the earlier condemnations were culture-bound (n. 4). The letter acknowledges that the Bible was composed in many different epochs with great cultural and historical diversity and that the church today addresses the gospel to a world which differs in many ways from ancient days (n. 5). In the light of this recognition of historical consciousness one is not prepared for the opening sentence of the next paragraph: "What should be noticed is that, in the presence of such remarkable diversity, there is nevertheless a clear consistency within the scriptures themselves on the moral issue of homosexual behaviour" (n. 5). Historical consciousness is mentioned only to deny it in practice.

The "Instruction on Respect for Human Life in Its Origin and on the Dignity of Procreation" promulgated in 1987 appeals to the unchangeable and immutable laws of human nature. The laws are described as "inscribed in the very being of man and of woman" (II, B, n. 4). These laws are "inscribed in their persons and in their union" (Introduction, n. 5).

This instruction describes its own methodology as deductive: "The moral criteria for medical intervention in procreation are deduced from the dignity of human persons, of their sexuality, and of their origins" (II, B, n. 7). "A first consequence can be deduced from these principles" of the natural law (Introduction, n. 3). In summary these documents show little or no historical consciousness in their approach to questions of sexuality.

The Emphasis Is on Nature and Faculties Rather Than on the Person

In the official hierarchical teaching on sexuality the methodology gives much more significance to nature and faculties than it does to the person. This has been a constant complaint against the older Catholic methodology in sexual ethics which has led to its teaching on masturbation, artificial contraception, sterilization, artificial insemination, homosexual acts, etc.[34] The manuals of moral theology based their sexual ethics on the innate purpose and God-given structure and finality of the sexual faculty. The sexual faculty has a twofold purpose — procreation and love union. Every sexual actuation must respect that twofold finality, and nothing should interfere with this God-given purpose. The sexual act itself must be open to procreation and expressive of love. Such an understanding forms the basis of the Catholic teaching that masturbation, contraception, and artificial insemination even with the husband's seed are always wrong.[35]

The popular mentality often thought that Catholic opposition to artificial contraception was based on a strong pronatalist position. However, such is not the case. Catholic teaching has also condemned artificial insemination with the husband's seed which is done precisely in order to have a child. In my judgment this condemnation points up the problematic aspect in the methodology of Catholic sexual teaching — the sexual faculty can never be interfered with and the sexual act must always be open to procreation and expressive of love. This natural act must always be present. The last chapter developed the position of many theologians that for the good of the person or the good of the marriage one can and should interfere with the sexual faculty and the sexual act. I have claimed that the official teaching is guilty of physicalism by insisting that the human person cannot interfere with the physical, biological structure of the sexual faculty or the sexual act. There is no doubt that the official documents under discussion here continue to accept and propose this basic understanding.

The "Declaration on Sexual Ethics" points out that the sexual teaching of the Catholic Church is based "on the finality of the sexual act and on the principal criterion of its morality: it is respect for its finality that ensures the moral goodness of this act" (n. 5). Sexual sins are described often in this document as "abuses of the sexual faculty" (n. 6, also nn. 8, 9). The nature of the sexual faculty and of the sexual act and not the person form the ultimate moral criterion in matters of sexual morality.

The letter on homosexuality cites the earlier "Declaration on Sexual Ethics" to point out that homosexual acts are deprived of their essential and indispensable finality and are intrinsically disordered (n. 3). This letter points out that it is only within marriage that the use of the sexual faculty can be morally good (n. 7). However, there does seem to be a development in this letter in terms of a greater appeal to personalism. The teaching claims to be based on the reality of the human person in one's spiritual and physical dimensions (n. 2). There are more references to the human person throughout this document than in the earlier declaration, but the change is only verbal. The methodology is ultimately still based on the nature of the faculty and of the act, which are then assumed to be the same thing as the person.

The instruction on some aspects of bioethics is very similar to the letter on homosexuality in this regard. There are references to the "intimate structure" of the conjugal act and to the conjugal act as expressing the self-gift of the spouses and their openness to the gift of life. The document also appeals to the meaning and values which are expressed in the language of the body and in the union of human persons (II, B, n. 4). Thus the terms, the finality of the faculty and of the act and the abuse of the sexual faculty, are not used, but the basic teaching remains the same. There are many more references to the person and to the rights of persons than in the earlier documents, but the change remains verbal and does not affect the substance of the teaching.

Ethical Model

There can be no doubt that the documents in official Catholic teaching on sexuality employ the law model as primary. The "Declaration on Sexual Ethics" in its discussion of ethical methodology insists on the importance of the divine law — eternal, objective, and universal — whereby God orders, directs, and governs the entire universe (n. 3). This document bases its teaching on the "existence of immutable laws inscribed in the constitutive elements of human nature and which are revealed to be identical in all beings endowed with reason" (n. 4). Throughout the introductory comments there is no doubt whatsoever that this declaration follows a legal model:

> Since sexual ethics concern certain fundamental values of human and Christian life, this general teaching equally applies to sexual

ethics. In this domain there exist principles and norms which the church has always unhesitatingly transmitted as part of her teaching, however much the opinions and morals of the world may have been opposed to them. These principles and norms in no way owe their origin to a certain type of culture, but rather to knowledge of the divine law and of human nature. They therefore cannot be considered as having become out of date or doubtful under the pretext that a new cultural situation has risen. (n. 5)

The "Letter to the Bishops of the Catholic Church on the Pastoral Care of Homosexual Persons" is by its very nature more concerned with pastoral care than with an explanation of the moral teaching and the ethical model employed in such teaching (n. 2). However, the occasional references found in this pastoral letter indicate the deontological model at work. There are frequent references to the will of God, the plan of God, and the theology of creation. Traditional Catholic natural law is the basis for this teaching. The teaching of scripture on this matter is called "theocratic law" (n. 6).

The recent instruction on bioethics definitely employs a deontological ethical model:

> Thus the Church once more puts forward the divine law in order to accomplish the work of truth and liberation. For it is out of goodness — in order to indicate the path of life — that God gives human beings his commandments and the grace to observe them. . . . (Introduction, n. 1)
>
> The natural moral law expresses and lays down the purposes, rights, and duties which are based upon the bodily and spiritual nature of the human person. Therefore this law cannot be thought of as simply a set of norms on the biological level; rather it must be defined as the rational order whereby the human being is called by the Creator to direct and regulate one's life and action and in particular to make use of one's own body. (Introduction, n. 3)

This document also cites the following quotation from *Mater et Magistra*: "The transmission of human life is entrusted by nature to a personal and conscious act and as such is subject to the all-holy laws of God: immutable and inviolable laws which must be recognized and observed" (Introduction, n. 4). Biomedical science and technology have grown immensely in the last few years, but "science and technology require, for their own intrinsic meaning, an unconditional respect for the fundamental criteria of the moral law" (Introduction, n. 2).

A very significant practical difference between a law model and a relationality-responsibility model is illustrated by the teaching proposed in these documents. In a legal model the primary question is the existence of law. If something is against the law, it is wrong; if there is no law against it, it is acceptable and good. Within such a perspective there is very little gray area. Something is either forbidden or permitted. Within a relationality-responsibility model there are more gray areas. Here one recognizes that in the midst of complexity and specificity one cannot always claim a certitude for one's moral positions.

The contemporary official Catholic teaching on social issues with its relationality-responsibility model recognizes significant gray areas. *Octogesima Adveniens* acknowledges the pluralism of options available and the need for discernment. The two recent pastoral letters of the United States Roman Catholic bishops on peace and the economy well illustrate such an approach. The documents make some very particular judgments, but they recognize that other Catholics might in good conscience disagree with such judgments. The bishops' letters call for unity and agreement on the level of principles, but they recognize that practical judgments on specific issues cannot claim with absolute certitude to be the only possible solution. The pastoral letter on peace, for example, proposes that the first use of nuclear weapons is always wrong but recognizes that other Catholics in good conscience might disagree with such a judgment.[36]

In the contemporary official Catholic teaching on sexual issues there is little or no mention of such gray areas. Something is either forbidden or permitted. Even in the complex question of bioethics the same approach is used. Certain technologies and interventions are always wrong; others are permitted. Thus the very way in which topics are treated— namely, either forbidden or permitted—indicates again that a legal model is at work in the hierarchical sexual teaching.

The thesis and the conclusions of this chapter are somewhat modest, but still very significant. There can be no doubt that there are three important methodological differences between hierarchical Roman Catholic teaching on social morality and the official hierarchical teaching on sexual morality. Whereas the official social teaching has evolved so that it now employs historical consciousness, personalism, and a relationality-responsibility ethical model, the sexual teaching still emphasizes classicism, human nature and faculties, and a law model of ethics. The ramifications of these conclusions are most significant, but they go beyond the scope of this study.

NOTES

1. Pope Leo XIII, *Rerum Novarum*, in Etienne Gilson, ed., *The Church Speaks to the Modern World: The Social Teachings of Leo XIII* (Garden City, NY: Doubleday Image Books, 1954), pp. 200-244.

2. Pope Pius XI, *Quadragesimo Anno*, in Terence P. McLaughlin, ed., *The Church and the Reconstruction of the Modern World: The Social Encyclicals of Pope Pius XI* (Garden City, NY: Doubleday Image Books, 1957), pp. 218-278.

3. Pope John XXIII, *Mater et Magistra*, in David J. O'Brien and Thomas A. Shannon, eds., *Renewing the Earth: Catholic Documents on Peace, Justice, and Liberation* (New York: Paulist Press, 1977), pp. 44-116.

4. Pope Paul VI, *Octogesima Adveniens*, in O'Brien and Shannon, *Renewing the Earth*, pp. 347-383.

5. Pope John Paul II, *Laborem Exercens*, in Gregory Baum, *The Priority of Labor* (New York: Paulist Press, 1982), pp. 95-152.

6. E.g., Pope Leo XIII, *Diuturnum*, in Gilson, *The Church Speaks to the Modern World*, pp. 140-161.

7. I have developed in greater detail this shift to historical consciousness as well as the shift to personalism in my *Directions in Catholic Social Ethics* (Notre Dame, IN: University of Notre Dame Press, 1985), pp. 6-22.

8. Gilson, *The Church Speaks to the Modern World*, p. 218.

9. For an interpretation that sees somewhat more continuity between Pope Pius XI and his successors see John F. Cronin, *Social Principles and Economic Life*, rev. ed. (Milwaukee: Bruce, 1964), pp. 130-140.

10. *Pacem in Terris*, nn. 39-45, 75-79, 126-129, 142-145, in

O'Brien and Shannon, *Renewing the Earth*, pp. 133-135, 143, 154, 158-159.

11. *Octogesima Adveniens*, n. 4, in ibid., pp. 353, 354.

12. *Octogesima Adveniens*, n. 22, in ibid., p. 364.

13. John Courtney Murray, "The Church and Totalitarian Democracy," *Theological Studies* 13 (1952): 525-563.

14. John Francis Maxwell, *Slavery and the Catholic Church* (London: Barry Rose Publishers, 1975), pp. 78, 79; Joseph D. Brokhage, *Francis Patrick Kenrick's Opinion on Slavery* (Washington: Catholic University of America Press, 1955).

15. John Courtney Murray, *The Problem of Religious Freedom* (Westminster, MD: Newman Press, 1965), pp. 52-66; Fr. Refoulé, "L'Église et les libertés de Léon XIII à Jean XXIII," *Le Supplément* 125 (mai 1978): 243-259.

16. McLaughlin, *The Chruch and the Reconstruction of the Modern World*, pp. 299-402.

17. Arthur F. McGovern, *Marxism: An American Christian Perspective* (Maryknoll, NY: Orbis Books, 1980), pp. 90-131.

18. *Mater et Magistra*, nn. 212-265, in O'Brien and Shannon, *Renewing the Earth*, pp. 102-114.

19. *Pacem in Terris*, nn. 35, 36, in ibid., p. 132.

20. *Pacem in Terris*, nn. 11-34, in ibid., pp. 126-132.

21. "Declaration on Religious Freedom," in ibid., pp. 285-306.

22. John Courtney Murray, "Vers une intelligence du développement de la doctrine de l'Église sur la liberté religieuse," in J. Hamer and Y. Congar, eds., *Vatican II: La liberté religieuse, declaration 'Dignitatis humanae personae'* (Paris: Éditions du Cerf, 1967), pp. 111-147.

23. *Octogesima Adveniens*, n. 22, in O'Brien and Shannon, *Renewing the Earth*, p. 364.

24. E.g., Marcellinus Zalba, *Theologiae Moralis Summa*, I: *Theologia Moralis Fundamentalis* (Madrid: Biblioteca de Autores Cristianos, 1952).

25. Thomas Aquinas, *Summa Theologiae, Pars I^a II^{ae}* (Rome: Marietti, 1952).

26. *Pacem in Terris*, nn. 1-5, in O'Brien and Shannon, *Renewing the Earth*, pp. 124, 125.

27. *Pacem in Terris*, nn. 6, 7, in ibid., pp. 125, 126.

28. *Octogesima Adveniens*, n. 42, in ibid., p. 375.

29. *Octogesima Adveniens*, n. 37, in ibid., p. 371.

30. *Octogesima Adveniens*, nn. 47-52, in ibid., pp. 378-382.

31. Congregation for the Doctrine of the Faith, "Declaration on Sexual Ethics," *Origins* 5 (1976): 485-494. References to this and

the subsequent documents will be to the official paragraph numbers. These documents are also available from the Publications Office, National Conference of Catholic Bishops, 1312 Massachusetts Ave. NW, Washington, DC 20005.

32. Congregation for the Doctrine of the Faith, "Letter to the Bishops of the Catholic Church on the Pastoral Care of Homosexual Persons," *Origins* 16 (1986): 377-382.

33. Congregation for the Doctrine of the Faith, "Instruction on Respect for Human Life in Its Origin and on the Dignity of Procreation," *Origins* 16 (1987): 697-711.

34. Luigi Lorenzetti, "Tramissione della vita humana: da un'etica della natura ad un'etica della persona," *Rivista di Teologia Morale* 18, n. 71 (1986): 117-129.

35. E.g., Marcellinus Zalba, *Theologiae Moralis Summa*, II: *Tractatus De Mandatis Dei et Ecclesiae* (Madrid: Biblioteca de Autores Cristianos, 1953), pp. 314-420.

36. United States Catholic Bishops, "The Challenge of Peace: God's Promise and Our Response," *Origins* 13 (1983): 2, 3.

6: Ethical Principles of Catholic Social Teaching in the United States Bishops' Letter on the Economy

Catholic social teaching has had a long history. Since the thirteenth century Thomistic thought has served as the basis for Catholic aproaches to society and the social order. Ever since Pope Leo XIII's encyclical *Rerum Novarum* (1891) there has existed a body of official Catholic social teaching proposed by the popes and later by the Second Vatican Council and the Synod of Bishops. There have been developments in this teaching over the years, but the principles and approach based on the thought of Thomas Aquinas (d. 1274) still play an important role in contemporary Catholic social thought and teaching. Other strands have developed in the church in varying degrees of relationship to the official church documents, but this discussion will concentrate on official Catholic social teaching. The most significant elements of the Catholic social teaching will now be examined to provide a background for understanding and interpreting the pastoral letter on the economy issued by the Roman Catholic bishops of the United States.

First, the Catholic understanding of society in general and the state in particular proposes a middle ground approach between the extremes of individualism and of collectivism. Human beings are by nature social and thus destined to live together in political society. The state is a natural society based on human nature itself. Such a position is distinguished from a Lutheran understanding which sees the state as an order of preservation established by God to keep sinful human beings from killing one another. The Catholic understanding also rejects all contract theories which see the state emerging from a contract freely entered into by autonomous individuals. At the same time the Catholic approach avoids a collectivism which subordinates the individual to the good of the state or the collectivity. The individual retains one's basic rights but finds in society and in political society what is necessary to truly achieve one's humanity. The end of the state is the common good, but the common good does not deny the basic goods and rights of the individual person. The common good ultimately redounds to the good of the individual.[1]

Perhaps Catholic theology has not given enough importance at times to the factor of coercion, but in the Thomistic understanding coercion is not of the essence of the state. Human beings before the fall and even angels live in political societies and need someone to direct them to the common good.[2] By belonging to political society the individual person does not lose one's freedom and suffer coercion. The analogy of an orchestra can well illustrate the basic Catholic understanding of the state. The director leads the various members to achieve the common good — a beautiful harmonious sound that could not be achieved by individuals alone. The individual members in responding to the director are not coerced against their will but rather play their particular roles in achieving the ultimate sound which can be produced only if many individuals work together for the common good.

The traditional Catholic understanding of the state thus stands midway between the extremes of individualism and collectivism. Individualism so stresses the individual that it fails to recognize the social nature of all human beings and that social and even political communities are natural to all humankind. Collectivism so stresses the collectivity that it fails to recognize and protect the basic dignity and rights of the individual. Historically, Catholic social thought has condemned collectivism and laissez-faire capitalism (although the condemnation of collectivism was stronger in some senses). Until recently this middle-way approach often resulted in the call for a third way, midway between capitalism and collectivism. However, in the last few decades there has been much less talk about such a detailed third way which often went under the name of corporatism or solidarism. In more contemporary usage this Catholic understanding has been employed to criticize the existing political and economic approaches.

Second, the principle of subsidiarity governs the role and activity of the state. Within society there exist not only the state and individuals but also many intermediate groups, associations, and institutions such as schools, the press, churches, labor unions, business associations, and so on. (Perhaps this is the best place to note that the traditional Catholic approach to the state does not recognize the different levels of political authority existing on the local, state, and national levels.) As early as 1891 Pope Leo XIII realized the need for state intervention to prevent injury not only to the common good but also to the interest of particular groups or classes if there were no other way to prevent this injury.[3] In 1931 Pope Pius XI in his encyclical *Quadragesimo Anno* enunciated the principle of subsidiarity:

> It is a fundamental principle of social philosophy, fixed and unchangeable, that one should not withdraw from individuals and commit to the community what they can accomplish by their own enterprise and industry. So, too, it is an injustice and at the same time a grave evil and a disturbance of right order to transfer to the larger and higher collectivity functions which can be performed and provided for by lesser and subordinate bodies. Inasmuch as every social activity should, by its very nature, prove a help to members of the body social, it should never destroy or absorb them.[4]

The state thus exists as a help (*subsidium*) for individuals and lesser associations, bodies, and institutions in society.

Some Catholics in the United States and elsewhere emphasized the negative phrasing of the principle of subsidiarity to insist on limiting the role of the state and decried the move toward statism in the United States.[5] However, in 1961 Pope

John XXIII in *Mater et Magistra* acknowleged the growing complexity and socialization (multiplication of social relationships) of modern life in general and of economic life in particular. Because of these growing relationships there are more and more demands upon the state to interfere in the economic order.[6] There can be some danger in this greater state involvement, but such growing state intervention does not necessarily mean that individual citizens will gravely be discriminated against or unfairly hindered. In keeping with the same understanding, the pastoral letter of the bishops affirms the positive role of government in the economic order, even recognizing the need for various types and kinds of economic planning but still rejecting a statist approach. The letter also points out that the principle of subsidiarity does not support the view that the government which governs least governs best.[7]

Third, the Catholic tradition has insisted that the principles of justice must govern economic life in society. The tradition has recognized three different types of justice — commutative, distributive, and legal, or social. Commutative justice governs the relationship between one individual and another. Distributive justice governs the relationship between the community as a whole or the state and individuals or smaller groups. Legal, or social, justice directs the relationship of individuals to the good of the community and of the state.[8] Commutative justice does not respect persons, is blind, and is characterized by arithmetic equality. If, for example, I borrow five dollars from you and five dollars from the richest person in the world, I owe both of you the same amount — five dollars. What I owe is totally independent of the person from whom I borrowed.

Distributive justice on the contrary does respect persons, is not blind, and is based on a proportional and not an arithmetic equality. In distributing goods and burdens the community in general and the state in particular must respect persons and their differences. The canons of distributive justice are complex, but great emphasis in distributing the goods of society is given to the basic needs of individuals, whereas in distributing burdens emphasis is placed on ability. Thus, for example, the Catholic tradition maintains that a just wage is more than what is freely agreed to by the worker and owner or manager. A just minimum wage is that which allows the worker and the worker's family to live a basically decent human existence. So, too, distributive justice is recognized as the need to distribute the goods of society so that all can enjoy that minimum of the goods of this world which is necessary for living a decent human life. On the other hand, this understanding of distributive justice argues for a progressive income tax in which those who have more will not only pay arithmetically more but will also pay a greater proportion of their income in taxation. In keeping with the Catholic understanding of the state which avoids both individualism and collectivism, distributive justice condemns both a total equality of goods as well as the assertion that the free forces of the marketplace should not be touched or controlled. All have a right to that basic minimum of the goods of this world which is necessary for living a decent human existence.

Since there are three different types of relationships involving the individual living in society with other human beings, Catholic social ethics has insisted that commutative, or individual, justice is not the only type of justice. Those who forget or downplay the social dimension of human existence tend to reduce all justice to commutative justice. The American ethos in general favors an almost exclusive emphasis on commutative justice, with the concomitant understanding that justice is blind and is characterized by mathematical equality. Of course there are times when commutative justice does come into play in human society. Just contracts, for example, must be observed. One must give a full day's work for a full day's pay. However, all justice cannot be reduced to commutative justice. Debate over affirmative action programs well illustrates the two different types of justice at work. Opponents of any affirmative action programs appeal to commutative justice, whereas the pastoral letter on the basis of distributive justice justifies some affirmative action programs (par. 167).

The third type of justice is now often called social justice, although the word was first introduced by Pope Pius XI in his 1931 encyclical *Quadragesimo Anno*. Within the tradition

Ethical Principles and the Bishops' Letter on the Economy 115

there is some discussion about the exact meaning of social justice, but the most common opinion, followed by the pastoral letter of the United States bishops, understands social justice to be the same as what had previously been called legal justice. Social justice or legal justice governs the relationship of the individual to the common good. Traditionally social justice called for obedience to just laws, payment of taxes, and contributions to the common good in general.

The pastoral letter creatively incorporates a comparatively new concept into social justice — the concept of participation (par. 68-78). For different reasons which will be discussed below Catholic theology has traditionally been fearful of freedom. Only in the face of totalitarian governments in the twentieth century did Catholic thought begin to emphasize the idea and importance of freedom. At the turn of the present century Catholic social thought was authoritarian at worst and paternalistic at best. Now the recognition of the freedom and dignity of the person (which is often associated more with the philosophical turn to the subject) calls for a greater participation of the individual in the life of society and in determining one's own life. No longer is it a question primarily of what society can do for and to the individual. The pastoral letter emphasizes the participation of the individual in the total life of society as a right based on social justice with the corresponding duty of society and all others to recognize and facilitate this right of participation. Such an understanding of social justice recognizes the contribution that all must make to the economic common good but especially emphasizes the right of the marginalized to participate in every way in the life of society.

Fourth, Catholic social teaching has developed in more recent times a theory of human rights including so-called economic rights. Earlier documents in the tradition tended to shy away from rights language because of the fear of individualism. The stress in Catholic social teaching before recent times was on duties rather than rights. The nineteenth-century church saw individualism as the great adversary and denied the freedom that served as a basis for such individualism. As the twentieth century progressed, the primary problem became totalitarianism, and Catholic social teaching ever more insistently stressed the freedom, dignity, and rights of the person. The recent social documents carry this even further with their insistence on equality and participation, two important themes in *Economic Justice for All.* It was Pope John XXIII in *Pacem in Terris* in 1963 who first explicitly developed the concept of human rights in official Catholic teaching.

> Beginning our discussion of human rights, we see that every human being has the right to life, to bodily integrity, and to the means that are suitable to the proper development of life; these are primarily food, clothing, shelter, rest, medical care, and finally the necessary social services. Therefore a human being also has the right to security in case of sickness, inability to work, widowhood, old age, unemployment, or in any other case in which one is deprived of the means of subsistence through no fault of one's own.[9]

Note that the recent development of human rights in Catholic social teaching is consonant with the individual and social anthropology which undergirds the Catholic understanding of the state. Human rights include not only political and civil rights but also economic rights. The general ethos in the United States often stresses the importance of political and civil rights (and did so long before Roman Catholicism did so) but forgets the existence of economic rights. These economic rights are also grounded in the dignity of the human person and are necessary for every human being.

Fifth, the understanding of private property in the Catholic tradition has always included an important social dimension which again has more heavily been emphasized in the last two decades. In early Christianity the social aspect of the goods of creation was strongly underscored. The very existence of private property was often understood as resulting primarily from the fall or the presence of sin in the world and not resulting from a demand of human nature as such. Thomas Aquinas, with his medieval synthesis, continued in this tradition of strongly recognizing the social aspect of property and morally limiting the way in which an individual could use property. At the end of the nineteenth century Leo XIII stressed the importance of the widespread ownership of private property as the means to protect people against the vagaries of the economic system. In this context Leo gave less emphasis and importance to the social aspect of property. However, more recent official church documents, beginning especially with the Pastoral Constitution on the Church in the Modern World of the Second Vatican Council, have emphasized the universal purpose of all created goods. The goods of creation exist to serve the needs of all human beings. Pope Paul VI in *Populorum Progressio* underscores the social aspect of property and maintains: "All other rights whatsoever including those of property and of free commerce are to be subordinated to this principle. They should not hinder but on the contrary favor its application. It is a grave and urgent social duty to redirect them to their primary finality."[10] The social finality of the goods of creation thus supports the requirement of distributive justice that all human beings have a right to a decent minimal standard of living.

Sixth, Catholic social teaching has recently insisted on a preferential option for the poor. This emphasis is intimately connected with a methodological shift which in the last two decades has proposed a more direct relationship between faith or the gospel and daily life. A strong gospel emphasis insists on the special place of and consideration for the poor. This option for the poor has been developed especially in the liberation theology of Latin America. The word "preferential" indicates that this option is not exclusive of the legitimate rights of others. However, such a preferential option for the poor gives a gospel foundation to the demand that all have a right to participate in the life of society and to have the basic minimum of goods necessary for decent human living.

The analysis of Catholic social teaching given above does not claim to be exhaustive but only attempts to point out the most important elements of the teaching as it provides a basis for the pastoral letter of the United States bishops on the economy. In the light of these principles and understandings no one should be surprised at the general approach and positions taken by the United States bishops in their letter. The bishops propose a reforming approach, rejecting a radical destruction of the existing economic system but also calling for many modifications within the system to overcome the individualistic emphases that are too often present today.

NOTES

1. Two classical explanations of the state in the Catholic tradition are Heinrich Rommen, *The State in Catholic Thought* (St. Louis: B. Herder, 1945) and Jacques Maritain, *Man and the State* (Chicago: University of Chicago Press, 1951).

2. Thomas Aquinas, *Summa Theologiae: Prima Pars* (Rome: Marietti, 1952), q. 96, a.4.

3. Pope Leo XIII, *Rerum Novarum*, par. 36, in Etienne Gilson, ed., *The Church Speaks to the Modern World: The Social Teachings of Leo XIII* (Garden City, NY: Doubleday, 1954), pp. 224-225.

4. Pope Pius XI, *Quadragesimo Anno*, par. 79, in Terence P. McLaughlin, ed., *The Social Encyclicals of Pope Pius XI* (Garden City, NY: Doubleday, 1957), p. 247.

5. Benjamin L. Masse, *Justice for All: An Introduction to the Social Teaching of the Catholic Church* (Milwaukee: Bruce, 1964), p. 77.

6. Pope John XXIII, *Mater et Magistra*, par. 54, in David J. O'Brien and Thomas A. Shannon, eds., *Renewing the Earth: Catholic Documents on Peace, Justice and Liberation* (Garden City, NY: Doubleday, 1977), p. 77.

7. National Conference of Catholic Bishops, *Economic Justice for All: Pastoral Letter on Catholic Social Teaching and the U.S. Economy* (Washington, DC: National Conference of Catholic Bishops, 1986), par. 124; 312-321. Since the letter has appeared in many places, references here and in the text will be to the official paragraph numbers.

8. For a similar understanding of the tradition see Joseph Pieper, *The Four Cardinal Virtues* (Notre Dame, IN: University of Notre Dame Press, 1966), pp. 43-113; Daniel C. Maguire, "The Primacy of Justice in Moral Theology," *Horizons* 10 (1983): 72-85. For a different reading of the tradition which sees legal justice as a general virtue see Jeremiah Newman, *Foundations of Justice* (Cork, Ireland: Cork University Press, 1954).

9. Pope John XXIII, *Pacem in Terris*, par. 11, in O'Brien-Shannon, *Renewing the Earth*, p. 126.

10. Pope Paul VI, *Populorum Progressio*, par. 22, in ibid., p. 320.

7: Official Catholic Social Teaching and the Common Good

Official Catholic social teaching in the modern era is usually understood as beginning with the social encyclicals of Pope Leo XIII at the end of the nineteenth century, especially the encyclical *Rerum Novarum*. Other benchmark documents which are usually included in this tradition are the following: Pope Pius XI's *Quadragesimo Anno* (1931); Pope John XXIII's *Mater et Magistra* (1961) and *Pacem in Terris* (1963); the Pastoral Constitution on the Church in the Modern World and the Declaration on Religious Freedom of the Second Vatican Council (1965); Pope Paul VI's *Populorum Progressio* (1967) and *Octogesima Adveniens* (1971); the Synod of Bishops' *Justitia in Mundo* (1971); Pope John Paul II's *Laborem Exercens* (1981).[1]

Modern official Catholic social teaching began with Pope Leo XIII, who also presided over the renewal of Thomistic philosophy in Catholic schools and scholarship. Thomas Aquinas was made the patron of Catholic theology and philosophy, which, according to the pope, were to be taught in line with the method, the principles, and the teaching of Thomas Aquinas. Thomistic theology was understood to be the perennial philosophy which undergirded Catholic theology and self-understanding.[2]

In this context Pope Leo XIII obviously based his social morality on Thomistic teachings and principles. A very central element in Thomistic political ethics is the concept of the common good, which deals with the fundamental question of the nature of political society and the relationship between

119

the individual and society. The common good is the end or the purpose of society, but the common good ultimately redounds to the good of the individuals involved. In this Thomistic concept the human being is by nature social, and civil and political society are natural. The individual's quest for perfection as well as the weakness and incompleteness of the human being call upon the individual to live in society, including political society. Thus society and the state are based on human nature. The pre-Vatican II papal documents, as one might expect, do not go into the philosophical grounding of the common good in great depth, but the early encyclicals use this understanding of the individual and society to condemn the two positions of individualistic liberalism on the one hand and collectivism on the other. The communitarian and social nature of the individual serves as the basis for the principles and more specific applications made in the official Catholic social teaching. Thus, for example, the principle of subsidiarity sees the role of the state as a help (*subsidium*) to enable individuals and lesser groups in society to do and accomplish what they can do. The state should not take over what can be done on the level of the individual or of lesser groupings in society, but at times the state must intervene and act for the good of all concerned.

In explaining the official Catholic social teaching commentators emphasized the Thomistic foundation of this teaching and developed the understanding of the common good, the role of the individual in society, and the fact that the state is a natural society based on human nature as social and not on sin and evil. The well-known book of Calvez and Perrin originally published in French in 1959 well illustrates the understanding of the Thomistic teaching on the individual, society, and the common good as the basis for official Catholic social teaching.[3] There would seem to be little or no argument against the position that official Catholic social teaching up to the time of the Second Vatican Council (1965) gave great importance to the concept of the common good and generally accepted the Thomistic foundations of this teaching.

I

A case can be made for the position that since Vatican II official Catholic social teaching has not given that significant and important a role to the concept of the common good, especially as rooted in Thomistic thought. Four generic reasons connected with official Catholic social teachings since Vatican II can be proposed to support this thesis:

1) Thomistic natural-law method no longer is the primary basis of Catholic social teaching and ethics;

2) The teaching itself incorporates elements that seem to be in opposition to the common-good tradition;

3) The documents do not explicitly give that much attention to the common good;

4) Catholic social thought as developed by contemporary theologians seems to have neglected the concept of the common good.

First, the methodology of the official Catholic social teaching since the Pastoral Constitution on the Church in the Modern World of Vatican II has definitely changed from the natural-law methodology employed in the earlier documents. There are two significant methodological developments that have taken place in the official Catholic social teaching since Vatican II. These two developments might be generally described as the theological and philosophical aspects of the methodology of social ethics.

The older documents were based almost totally on the natural-law approach which prescinded from the supernatural, grace, faith, and the gospel.[4] However, the recent documents appeal very often to the gospel. Action on behalf of justice is seen to be a constitutive dimension of the preaching of the gospel and the mission of the church for the redemption of humankind.[5] These documents very correctly recognize that faith and the gospel, and not only reason and natural law, have something to say about political and economic realities, and about social and political ethics. However, the gospel must always be mediated in and through the human. This theological aspect of methodology can be seen as a matter of the sources of ethical wisdom and knowledge for the Christian.

A second methodological change concerns the philosophical understanding of human reason and human nature. Chapter five developed at length three significant methodological changes within official Catholic social teaching — the shifts to historical consciousness, to personalism, and to a relationality-responsibility ethical model. Historical consciousness gives more importance to the individual, the contingent, the particular, the historical, and the changing, and is associated with a more inductive methodology. Since the Pastoral Constitution on the Church in the Modern World in 1965 ecclesiastical documents have given greater emphasis to the signs of the times and have developed a more inductive methodology. Thus, for example, *Octogesima Adveniens*, which is perhaps the most radical of recent documents in its methodology, recognizes that in the midst of widely varying situations throughout the world it is neither the ambition nor the mission of the pope to put forth a solution which has universal validity. Local Christian communities must in the light of the gospel and the social teaching of the church discern the options and the commitments that are called for in their situations (par. 4, in O'Brien and Shannon, *Renewing the Earth*, pp. 353-354). *Octogesima Adveniens* thus illustrates the influence of historical mindedness in contemporary official Catholic social teaching.

A second changed aspect of the philosophical understanding of the human being has been the greater emphasis on personalism and all that is connected with it, such as human rights. This personalism is present in all the recent documents and is the hallmark of Pope John Paul II's *Laborem Exercens*. It can be maintained that Pope John Paul II has tended to move away from the historical consciousness of Paul VI, but there is no doubt about his emphasis on personalism. Two important examples of this contemporary personalism developed in *Octogesima Adveniens* are the aspirations to equality and to participation (par. 22ff, in O'Brien and Shannon, *Renewing the Earth*, pp. 364ff). A third shift in the more philosophical understanding of the methodology of Catholic social teaching involves the adoption of a relationality-responsibility ethical model. Such a model is very consistent with the changes to historical consciousness and to personalism.

These three developments in the understanding of the human differ from the earlier approach based on the Scholastic notion of natural law. Thus, the understanding of the human and human reality found in the recent documents differs somewhat from the older natural-law approach. The theological and metaphysical bases for the common-good approach are no longer the same as those proposed in earlier documents.

Second, the newer documents introduce elements and approaches that seem to replace or even go against the basic concept of the common good. The more recent documents emphasize equality, but the classical Catholic common-good concept was fearful that equality could too readily be seen as an individualism which destroys the organic unity of society. The image or metaphor of the body with its many different parts was often used to describe the unity of the state with unequal functions and operations contributing to the good of the whole. The stress on such concepts as rights, freedom, and participation seem to be opposed to the classical Catholic notion of the common good. More recently the preferential option for the poor and solidarity with the poor have come to the fore. By emphasizing a part rather than the whole, these expressions seem to go against the very nature of the common good.

Third, an examination of the more recent documents reveals that the common good is not a central theme in many of these writings. There is no real development of the common good in John Paul II's *Laborem Exercens* or the synodal document *Justice in the World*. However, *Octogesima Adveniens* devotes a short section to political society and appeals to the common good as the basis for a condemnation of both individualism and collectivism (par. 23-25, in O'Brien and Shannon, *Renewing the Earth*, pp. 364-366). The Pastoral Constitution on the Church in the Modern World of Vatican II discusses political life in the fourth chapter of the second part and relies on the fundamental concept of the common good. In this connection it is important to remember that even the earlier documents in the body of official Catholic social teaching did not develop the concept of the common good in great philosophical depth or detail. Such an approach is really not that appropriate in documents destined for all and not merely for academics and specialists. Yes, the common good is occasionally mentioned in these documents, but it does not seem to play a very central role in them.

Fourth, the commentaries on contemporary Catholic social teaching and Catholic philosophy in general no longer give great importance to the concept of the common good. A check of the *Catholic Periodical and Literature Index* is most revealing. There is no entry under "common good" from volume 13 (1965-66) to the present. There are many entries under "common good" in volume 12 (1963-64) and in the preceding volumes. This certainly indicates that Catholic scholars are not paying much attention to the notion of the common good. A comparison of commentaries on Catholic social teaching points in the same direction. As already indicated, Calvez and Perrin writing in 1959 included a long chapter on persons in society with a section on the common good. Donal Dorr, in his recent *Option for the Poor: A Hundred Years of Vatican Social Teaching*, has no development of the concept of the common good, and the term does not even appear in the index.[6] Thus, the case can be made that recent official Catholic social teaching has moved away from the emphasis of the earlier social teaching on the common good and its importance for political and social teaching.

II

The opening section of this chapter developed the reasons for maintaining that recent official Catholic social teaching has downplayed the role and concept of the common good. This section will try to indicate that such a picture is not totally accurate. Yes, there are some discontinuities with the earlier teachings, but there is also continuity on the fundamental ideas involved in the traditional understanding of the common good. Second, some of the discontinuity with earlier Catholic social teaching can be explained by the recognition that the concrete content of the common good by its very nature is subject to change and development. Third, some developments which appear to go against the concept of the common good are not necessarily opposed to this notion. Each of these three parts will now be developed in greater detail.

Continuity with the Common-Good Tradition

First, official Catholic social teaching since Vatican Council II has continued to uphold the basic and essential aspects of the common-good tradition. As mentioned above, the concept of the common good is highlighted when these documents discuss political life. This tradition is rooted in an anthropology that stresses the social nature of humankind and results in an approach to political society which tries to avoid both extremes of individualism and collectivism. There can be no doubt that this basic meaning continues to be at the heart of recent Catholic social teaching. This teaching serves as the basis for an attack on individualism, which does not recognize the social aspect of human beings. The drafters of the bishops' pastoral letter on the United States economy recognize that the major difference between Catholic social teaching and the United States ethos is the latter's emphasis on individualism. There can be no doubt that the church has learned many things from the United States' experience, but it properly points out the dangers of individualism in our society. At the same time recent Catholic teaching with its greater emphasis on personalism strongly opposes any collectivism which subordinates the person to the collectivity.

The more recent documents do not call the state a natural society, but they do insist that the state is basically something good and has a positive function. Here again is a conviction of Catholic social teaching which at times differs sharply from the approach which sees government as something evil and believes that the government which governs least is the best form of government. The state is not something negative that unduly restricts human freedom, but the state has the positive function of promoting justice and true freedom for all.

The contemporary Catholic social teaching continues to put

into practice the principle of subsidiarity which is intrinsically connected with the core of the common-good tradition. This principle recognizes a rightful role for individual persons and for voluntary associations in society as well as for the state itself. This practical principle attempts to put flesh and blood on the basic approach which tries to avoid both individualism and collectivism. The state should do everything possible to support and help the individuals and the smaller voluntary societies to do what they can. However, at times the state itself must intervene to accomplish what the individuals and smaller groups cannot do.

Thus, in my judgment there can be no doubt that recent official Catholic social teaching continues to maintain the basic core and central aspects of the common-good tradition. In a sense this should not be surprising, for the Thomistic common-good tradition never really saw itself as an absolute but as an understanding of the basic biblical and Christian vision in the light of the circumstances of the time. That basic biblical vision should always be controlling and guiding. Of course, it is possible to interpret the biblical view in different ways as is evident in the difference between the classical Lutheran and Roman Catholic approaches. However, the Catholic tradition has always interpreted the biblical vision as stressing the communal and social dimension of human existence. Even in political society we are not merely individuals, but we are a people and a community. Robert Bellah and the other co-authors of *Habits of the Heart* have recognized that the biblical vision is communitarian and opposed to the individualism so often prevalent in contemporary United States society.[7] With that same controlling biblical vision contemporary Catholic social teaching continues to emphasize the social and communitarian dimension of human existence in the political sphere.

Second, there can be no doubt that there have been some changes and developments in the understanding and content of the common good in the more recent official Catholic social teaching. The fact of such change and development, however, should not be suprising.

Even before Vatican II there were changes in the under-

standing of the common good as found in official Catholic
social teaching and in Catholic philosophy and theology. The
best illustration of this development is the emphasis on personalism in the period of the 50s and 60s. In Thomistic
philosophy in the 1940s an interesting debate occurred on this
same issue. Jacques Maritain had been stressing the personal-
istic aspect of Thomistic thought and showing how it was
compatible with more contemporary emphasis on democratic
forms of government.[8] However, some other Thomists objected that by stressing personalism Maritain was denying the
primacy of the common good in Thomistic political ethics.[9]
This discussion is mentioned here only to point out that there
were changes and developments in the understanding of the
elements of the common good even before Vatican II.

The two previous chapters have indicated that the emphasis
on personalism also grew in the papal documents as the twentieth century progressed. The dignity, freedom, and even
rights of the human person became more central realities in
the papal understanding of the content of the common good.
Nineteenth-century Catholic social teaching strongly opposed
the excesses of individualistic liberalism, but in the twentieth
century the greater danger was now coming from the rise of
totalitarianism. As a result Catholic social teaching began to
defend the dignity, freedom, and rights of the individual.
Only in *Pacem in Terris* in 1963 does there appear the first
full-blown treatment of human rights in the Catholic social
tradition (par. 9-37, in O'Brien and Shannon, *Renewing the
Earth*, pp. 126-133). Vatican II sees this emphasis on human
dignity and rights as part of the common good.

Even before Vatican II there was a recognition that the
content of the common good is bound to change. The article
on the common good in *The New Catholic Encyclopedia* was
written before the documents of Vatican II were issued, but
it concludes with the following recognition: "It is simply impossible to define the common good in a final way irrespec-
tive of the changing social conditions."[10] The Pastoral Constitution on the Church in the Modern World refers to "the
dynamically conceived common good" (par. 74, in O'Brien
and Shannon, *Renewing the Earth*, p. 254).

Obviously a major shift has come about in the understanding of political life in Catholic social teaching from the time of Pope Leo XIII in the nineteenth century to the present. An even greater change marks the difference between the understanding of Thomas Aquinas and that of contemporary church documents. The older understanding saw society as structured from the top down, while contemporary ecclesiastical documents see political society as centered on the human person living in community with great emphasis on the dignity, freedom, and rights of the person. It is only natural that the concrete content of the common good will be different in these two diverse understandings of society. The next section will develop some of the more significant changes which have occurred in the contemporary official Catholic understanding of the common good.

Changes in the Content of the Common Good

One of the most significant developments in the Catholic tradition concerns the relationship between the temporal common good and the spiritual common good. This question was generally discussed under the rubric of the union or separation of church and state and the acceptance or denial of religious liberty. Only at Vatican II did Catholic teaching accept religious liberty. Many factors contributed to this change in Catholic social teaching, but a major aspect was the growing importance given to the freedom, rights, and dignity of the person. The state has no direct competency in matters of religion. The proponents of religious freedom at Vatican II in no way accepted the notion that the church and religion were private realities with no role in influencing human individual and social life. However, the newer approach saw that the common good of human political society did not call for the union of church and state.[11] In subsequent years the debate has shifted from the relationship of church and state to the relationship of church and society and how the church should address and be present to human existence in this world. But the Catholic Church today strongly recognizes that the temporal common good demands religious freedom and the so-called separation of church and state.

Another significant development concerns the precise end of the state and its function. Here there have been two significant developments which have existed simultaneously within the present teaching but have not been coordinated in that teaching itself. The first development arose in the context of the religious freedom debate and concerns the distinction between the common good and the public order. The state is only one part of the total civil society. Precisely because the contemporary Catholic understanding recognizes the freedom, dignity, and rights of individual persons and the role of lesser associations within society, the state can never be identified with the totality of society. The end of society is the common good, whereas the end of the state is much narrower — the public order. The Declaration on Religious Freedom accepts this distinction in the light of its recognition of the lesser role of government in the life of society (par. 6, 7, in O'Brien and Shannon, *Renewing the Earth*, pp. 296, 297). There is a public role for religion in affecting human society, but this area lies beyond the legitimate reach of government, which by definition is limited. Public order in this understanding is an order of justice, of public morality, and of public peace. I would add that the role of justice also includes social justice, so that the role of the state is not unduly limited. Despite the insistence on public order as the end of the state in the document on religious liberty, this concept is not developed in any other official church document after 1965.

In the discussion on religious liberty there was an insistence on a more limited role for the state precisely because the aspect of religion and its effect on society lie beyond the competency of the power of the state. At the same time the more recent official church documents, including those of Pope John XXIII in the early 1960s, insist on a greater role for the state than did the earlier documents. As mentioned before, these later documents still refer to the principle of subsidiarity, but now this principle is used to justify a greater role for the state than in the past. Pope John XXIII in *Mater et Magistra* still cautions against the danger of the state taking away the rightful role of individuals and voluntary associations, but he recognizes that public authorities are requested to intervene in a wide variety of economic affairs and are

called in a more extensive and organized way than hereto-
fore to adapt institutions, tasks, means, and procedures to
the common good (par. 54, in O'Brien and Shannon, *Renewing the Earth*, p. 63). These two emphases are not necessarily
incompatible, but there is need for the official teaching to
recognize both of them and to show how they are compatible. The danger is that in talking about the area of religious
liberty one will stress a lesser role for the state, whereas in
talking about social and economic concerns one will speak
about a greater role for the state.

Another important characteristic of the understanding of
the content of the common good in more recent church documents concerns the worldwide nature of the problems facing
humankind. In the beginning of *Populorum Progressio* Pope
Paul VI insists: "Today the principal fact we must recognize
is that the social question has become worldwide" (par. 3, in
O'Brien and Shannon, *Renewing the Earth*, p. 313). Subsequent
church documents in their treatment of the contemporary
issues well illustrate this fact. No question today can be discussed merely in terms of the problems affecting one country
or one area of the world alone. The obligations of the first
world vis-à-vis the third world are very significant. In this
context of the growing recognition of the solidarity of all
human beings in this world there is much less emphasis on
the common good within individual countries. The greater
emphasis on ecological problems throughout the world also
illustrates this same development. This very significant new
emphasis will of necessity tend to see all problems in terms
of the universal solidarity of all human beings in all parts of
the globe rather than in light of the common good of a particular nation.

The emphasis on personalism has had a great impact on
the concrete content and context of the common good. As
already mentioned, Catholic social teaching only recently has
developed the important concept of human rights. There can
be no doubt that this represents a significant change in Catholic self-understanding. The older tradition emphasized duties
and not rights. Some see in this development the proof that
contemporary Catholic social teaching is moving away from

the common-good tradition associated with Thomas Aquinas.[12] However, Vatican II sees this as a legitimate and necessary development of the concrete content of the common good in the light of changing circumstances.

Doubtless the Catholic tradition has learned much from the emphasis on human rights in the United States ethos, but to its credit the recent Catholic teaching also explicitly criticizes the individualistic tone of the rights tradition as often found in the United States. An emphasis on rights and freedom easily results in a one-sided individualism. While trying to appreciate the importance of fundamental human rights, contemporary Catholic social teaching has also attempted to avoid the dangers of excessive individualism. *Pacem in Terris* recognizes the need for duties as well as rights. In addition, Pope John XXIII insists on the existence of economic rights as well as political and civil rights. Economic rights recognize the social and communitarian aspects of human existence. People have rights to basic food, clothing, and shelter; society must protect and promote these rights.

The insistence on personalism has also stressed the primary importance of equality and participation. *Octogesima Adveniens* makes this point: "While scientific and technological progress continues to overturn man's surroundings, his patterns of knowledge, work, consumption and relationships, two aspirations persistently make themselves felt in these new contexts, and they grow stronger to the extent that he becomes better informed and better educated: the aspiration to equality and the aspiration to participation, two forms of man's dignity and freedom" (par. 22, in O'Brien and Shannon, *Renewing the Earth*, p. 364).

The recognition of the importance of equality raises some problems for the Catholic tradition. Traditionally Catholic social teaching did not give much importance to equality. An emphasis on equality was looked upon as inimical to the organic nature of political society and community. Within society as an organism each one had a different task and function to fulfill. Society needed the different functions and roles of different people. Here again one finds a new emphasis in the more recent social teaching which, without some nuances,

might go against a more traditional emphasis. A flat equalitarianism seems opposed to the communal and social nature
of human existence which has been a hallmark of the Catholic and Thomistic traditions. *Octogesima Adveniens* recognizes
the problem: "Without a renewed education and solidarity,
an overemphasis on equality can give rise to an individualism
in which each one claims one's own rights without wishing
to be answerable for the common good" (par. 23, in O'Brien
and Shannon, *Renewing the Earth*, p. 365). However, more
work needs to be done to indicate how the acceptance of
equality will not ultimately destroy the solidarity and communal nature of human social existence.

The emphasis on equality raises a somewhat related question concerning the relationship of recent Catholic social
teaching to its Thomistic roots and origins. What is the understanding of justice operative in the recent documents? The
traditional Thomistic understanding stressed distributive
justice according to which the burdens and goods of society
should be properly divided. In distributing goods, human need
constitutes a basic level or floor. All human beings have a
right to the basic goods of this world which are necessary
for a minimally decent level of human existence. Above and
beyond this basic minimum level for all there can be differences and inequalities connected to other titles such as labor,
creativity, scarcity, etc. The Thomistic tradition did not insist
on an equalitarian justice demanding total equality for all.[13]
The contemporary documents without a doubt give much
more emphasis to equality and point out the glaring inequalities of our age. However, as mentioned in chapter six, the
category of distributive justice and not equalitarian justice still
remains at the heart of recent social teaching. Other commentators put more emphasis on equalitarian justice.[14] Doubtless recent documents rightly stress equality, but the emphasis
is almost always nuanced in the official documents to speak
about the dangers of excessive or inappropriate or glaring
inequalities. As a result I think the concept of distributive
justice still plays the central role. Without a doubt distributive
justice is the controlling concept in the recent draft of the
bishops' pastoral letter on the United States economy.[15] The

older concept of distributive justice as well as the common good still exercises an important function in recent Catholic social teaching even though there have been significant developments.

Another development in the understanding of the common good in practice concerns the growing recognition of a somewhat more conflictual model of society. The common-good tradition sees all the members working together for the good of the whole, which ultimately redounds to the good of the individual. The emphasis in the past was often on harmonious cooperation. Now there is more emphasis on challenging the inequities among various parts of the world and within different sectors in the same national society. More recent church documents recognize a greater role for power in society by the oppressed and accept revolution as a last resort.[16] In my judgment a greater emphasis on human sinfulness as well as the realities of our modern world point to the recognition of more conflict in the political and social order than was recognized by the older Thomistic tradition. The recent documents rightly talk more about power and the need to overcome the powerlessness of so many people. In my judgment contemporary Catholic social teaching should give even greater recognition to a more conflictual model of existing society and the need for a more theoretical development of the understanding and role of power. Power and conflict can never become ultimate realities, but they do have a greater role in terms of tactics and strategies than has been recognized in the older Catholic social tradition.

Yes, there have been a number of important changes in the context and concrete content of the common good throughout the whole history of official Catholic social teaching. These developments have become even more prominent since 1961, but they in no way go against the basic thrust of the common-good tradition.

Newer Aspects and the Common-Good Tradition

The third point in this section concerns the discussion of those aspects in recent Catholic social teaching which might be opposed to the common-good tradition. The emphasis on inequalities in the modern world has already been discussed. The development in recent social teaching which seems at first sight somewhat opposed to the common-good tradition concerns the preferential option for the poor. Is such an option compatible with the common-good tradition or does it so emphasize a part that the whole suffers? In general I do not see the preferential option for the poor as opposed to the common-good tradition. Such an approach recognizes a more conflictual model of society. The language of powerlessness also supports this emphasis, but it does not necessarily deny that political society is natural for human beings and all must work for the common good. Note the emphasis on the *preferential* option for the poor as distinguished from an exclusive option for the poor which would definitely deny the common-good tradition. By preferring the poor one does not necessarily exclude all others in society.

The preferential option for the poor is putting into contemporary and even somewhat biblical language a point which was enshrined in the older Thomistic tradition's notion of distributive justice. Distributive justice insisted on a basic minimum necessary for all human beings. This fundamental floor or basic level had priority over other considerations. Such an understanding is also totally compatible with the traditional insistence which has become even more prevalent in contemporary times that the goods of creation exist to serve the needs of all. Thus the preferential option for the poor is in continuity with many of the emphases that have been a part of the Thomistic and Catholic social teaching traditions.

The emphasis on the preferential option for the poor without simultaneously downplaying the common good is analogous to what Leo XIII in *Rerum Novarum* said about the plight of workers and the poor. "Whenever the general interest, or any particular class, suffers or is threatened with harm which can in no other way be met or prevented, the public authority must step in to deal with it." "The richer class has many ways of shielding themselves and stand less in need of help from the State; whereas the mass of the poor have no resources of their own to fall back upon, and must chiefly depend upon the assistance of the State" (par. 36, 37, in Gilson, *The Pope Speaks to the Modern World*, pp. 225-226). A preferential concern or option for those worse off in no way destroys the basic understanding of the common good.

The first section of this chapter tried to make the case for saying that recent official Catholic social teaching has moved away from the concept of the common good. However, the second section has tried to prove that the basic realities of the common-good tradition are still found in contemporary Catholic social teaching. The common-good tradition itself recognized that the concrete content and context would change over time. An examination of the recent official teachings has tried to point out the more significant changes which have occurred, especially in more contemporary times. Nor can one maintain that the introduction of new emphases such as that of equality or the preferential option for the poor is opposed to the core of the common-good tradition.

The primary purpose of this study has been to analyze the understanding of the common good in the documents of official Catholic social teaching. This analysis, however, raises some significant questions for further study. To what extent should the contemporary documents make more explicit their dependence on basic notions of the Catholic tradition such as the common good? To what extent can the common-good tradition exist without all of its Thomistic metaphysical grounding? Without doubt the draft of the pastoral letter on the United States economy definitely appeals to the common good and bases its teaching explicitly on this concept. Also important questions need to be studied as a result of the developments that have occurred in the understanding of the content and context of the common good. How precisely can the recognition that human beings are by nature social and civil society is basically good be reconciled with the growing emphasis on freedom, equality, and rights? How much of a role should be given to power and conflict as strategies and tactics without destroying the common fabric of society? How is distributive justice related to the contemporary emphasis on equality?

NOTES

1. There are a number of unofficial collections containing many of these documents. See especially David J. O'Brien and Thomas A. Shannon, eds., *Renewing the Earth: Catholic Documents on Peace, Justice, and Liberation* (Garden City, NY: Doubleday Image Books, 1977); David M. Byers, ed., *Justice in the Marketplace: Collected Statements of the Vatican and the Unitd States Catholic Bishops on Economic Policy, 1981-1984* (Washington, DC: United States Catholic Conference, 1985). Future references to official documents will be to O'Brien and Shannon wherever possible.

2. Leo XIII, *Aeterni Patris*, in Etienne Gilson, ed., *The Pope Speaks to the Modern World: The Social Teachings of Leo XIII* (Garden City, NY: Doubleday Image Books, 1954), pp. 29-54.

3. Jean-Yves Calvez and Jacques Perrin, *The Church and Social Justice: The Social Teachings of the Popes from Leo XIII to Pius XII* (Chicago: Henry Regnery, 1961), pp. 101-132.

4. Calvez and Perrin, *The Church and Social Justice*, pp. 36-53.

5. 1971 Synod of Bishops, *Justitia in Mundo*, in O'Brien and Shannon, *Renewing the Earth*, p. 391.

6. Donal Dorr, *Option for the Poor: A Hundred Years of Vatican Social Teaching* (Maryknoll, NY: Orbis, 1983).

7. Robert N. Bellah et al., *Habits of the Heart: Individualism and Commitment in American Life* (Berkeley: University of California Press, 1985).

8. Jacques Maritain, *The Person and the Common Good* (New York: Charles Scribner's Sons, 1947; paperback ed., Notre Dame, IN: University of Notre Dame Press, 1966).

9. Charles DeKoninck, *De la primauté du bien commun* (Quebec: Éditions de l'Université Laval et Montreal: Fides, 1943); Jules A. Baisnee, "Two Catholic Critiques of Personalism," *The Modern Schoolman* 22 (1944-45): 59-74; I. Th. Eschmann, "In Defense of Jacques Maritain," *The Modern Schoolman* 22 (1944-45): 183-208; Charles DeKoninck, "In Defense of St. Thomas: A Reply to Father Eschmann's Attack on the Primacy of the Common Good," *Laval theologique et philosophique* 1, no. 2 (1945): 9-109; Yves R. Simon, "On the Common Good," *Review of Politics* 6 (1944): 530-533.

10. A. Nemetz, "Common Good," *New Catholic Encyclopedia*, 1967, IV, 15-19.

11. For a study of the debates at Vatican II see Richard J. Regan, *Conflict and Consensus: Religious Freedom and the Second Vatican Council* (New York: Macmillan, 1967).

12. Ernest L. Fortin, "The New Rights Theory and the Natural Law," *Review of Politics* 44 (1982): 590-612.

13. For a contemporary appreciation and application of the Thomistic tradition on justice see Daniel C. Maguire, *A New American Justice: Ending the White Male Monopolies* (Garden City, NY: Doubleday, 1980). However there is a dispute among contemporary Catholic thinkers. Some with Maguire see three particular kinds of justice — individual, legal or social, and distributive. For the opinion that legal justice is a general virtue and not a particular kind of justice see Normand Joseph Paulhus, "The Theological and Political Ideals of the Fribourg Union" (Ph.D. Diss., Boston College–Andover-Newton Theological Seminary, 1983).

14. E.g., Drew Christiansen, "On Relative Equality: Catholic Equalitarianism after Vatican II," *Theological Studies* 45 (1984): 651-675.

15. *Economic Justice for All: Pastoral Letter on Catholic Social Teaching and the U.S. Economy* (Washington, DC: National Conference of Catholic Bishops, 1986), par. 70, p. 36.

16. Congregation for the Doctrine of the Faith, *Instruction on Christian Freedom and Liberation* (Vatican City: Vatican Polyglot Press, 1986), par. 78, p. 47.

8: The United States and West German Bishops on Peace and War

This chapter attempts to analyze and compare from the perspective of moral theology the two pastoral letters of the West German bishops and of the United States bishops on peace, nuclear war, and deterrence. The first section will discuss some of the more significant differences between the two letters from a methodological perspective. The second section will examine the differences between the two letters on the important substantive issues of pacifism, the use of nuclear weapons, and nuclear deterrence. In the course of developing these two sections references will be made to the discussions which took place at two United States–West German symposia on Catholic teaching on war and peace held in 1985 and 1986 under the auspices of the scientific working group of the conference of German bishops on international affairs and the Woodstock Theological Center.

Methodological Differences

Both the West German and the United States bishops are writing out of the same Catholic tradition. Both give strong emphasis to official Catholic teaching and frequently cite papal teaching. However, there are significant differences between them. This section will discuss their different understandings of just-war theory, other methodological differences, and the different processes involved in writing the documents.

Just-War Theory

The most significant methodological issue in dealing with the ethical aspects of the question of peace and war concerns the basic theory or criteria employed to make moral judgments in this area. The Catholic tradition has developed the just-war theory, and it should not be surprising that both letters employ such a theory. However, there are significant differences in the way the two letters use this theory.

"Out of Justice, Peace," the West German bishops' letter, gives more emphasis to the historical development of the theory and even accentuates the changes and development that have occurred in the course of history.[1] The German letter even changes the name of the theory from the just war to the just defense in the light of more recent historical developments (86).

The United States letter does not give that much attention to the historical development but does spell out in very great detail all the criteria involved in the just-war theory (80-110).[2] The letter distinguishes between the *ius ad bellum*, why and where recourse to war is permissible, and the *ius in bello*, or the limitations put on the means used even in a just war. Seven conditions are spelled out as necessary to justify the recourse to war. However, the *ius in bello* puts a limitation on what can be done even in a just war.

There are two principles governing the *ius in bello* — the principle of discrimination and the principle of proportionality. These are proposed as two independent principles. The principle of discrimination requires that the just response to aggression "must be directed against unjust aggressors not against innocent people caught up in a war not of their own making" (104). The principle of discrimination "prohibits directly intended attacks on noncombatants and nonmilitary targets" (107). "The Challenge of Peace: God's Promise and Our Response," the United States letter, recognizes that questions are raised about the meaning of "intentional," "noncombatant," and "military" (107). According to this principle of discrimination the targeting of noncombatants and the execution of hostages are evil means in themselves and can be justified by no end whatsoever. However, even if the means is not evil in itself, the principle of proportionality comes into play. This principle of proportionality maintains that the advantages that will be achieved by using these means must not be disproportionate to the harms reasonably expected to follow from use (105).

Although the United States bishops develop at length both the *ius ad bellum* criteria and the *ius in bello* criteria, the major thrust of their analysis of nuclear war and deterrence rests on the *ius in bello* criteria. Comparatively little is said about the *ius ad bellum*. The ethical analysis in the letter is concerned with the limitations on nuclear use and deterrence prescribed by the principles of discrimination and proportionality presupposing the existence of a just war.

The West German letter is quite different. There is no detailed development of the criteria of the just-war theory. In discussing the development of the doctrine of just war (57-65) mention is made of the conditions necessary for a just war in Augustine, Aquinas, the Spanish theologians of the sixteenth century, the Scholastic and the neo-Scholastic theologians. However, there is no mention of the *ius in bello* in general or the principle of discrimination in particular as being involved in the historical development of the just-war theory. Nowhere in the letter do the West German bishops mention the principle of discrimination or noncombatant immunity. The letter (90) does recall the condemnation of total war and cites the famous sentence from Vatican II's Pastoral Constitution on the Church in the Modern World (n. 80): "Every act of war directed to the indiscriminate destruction of whole cities or vast areas with their inhabitants is a crime against God and man which merits firm and unequivocal condemnation." The letter subsequently paraphrases this teaching (151). For the United States bishops this condemnation of total war is based on the independent principle of discrimination. The West German bishops in their letter do not explicitly recognize such a principle. It would be possible to arrive at a condemnation of total war on the basis of the principle of proportionality. Such total war is disproportionate to any good that might come from it.

In their explicit discussion of deterrence the German bishops do discuss the question of means but never the principle of discrimination. In fact the means is a very important consideration, and "the methods chosen to pursue one's security policy should be measured in terms of the goal of preventing war" (143). In a very brief consideration of the weapons that can be used in a just war the letter mentions only the principle of the proportionality of the means as determining the morality of use (149).

It is thus very clear that in contrast to the United States letter the West German bishops do not explicitly employ the principle of discrimination. There is evidence that they do not accept the principle of discrimination as such but accept only the principle of proportionality as governing the use of military means.

The West German bishops give more emphasis to the *ius ad bellum* criteria in their analysis than do the United States bishops. The West German letter even calls the just-war theory the just-defense theory and proposes arguments to justify such defense. One legitimate criticism of the United States letter is that it never really develops in depth its rationale for defense and some deterrence. The West German bishops describe the two dangers confronting the world today as the danger to the freedom of nations and their citizens from totalitarian systems which disregard fundamental human rights and the second danger of the proliferation of armaments which might result in the catastrophe of nuclear war (130). These two dangers both justify and limit deterrence. In this context the letter calls for a continual confrontation with the ideological forces of Marxism-Leninism at the political, intellectual, and moral levels (131).

The insistence on the principle of discrimination as an important part of the *ius in bello* consideration is a central component of the letter issued by the United States bishops and distinguishes this letter from the West German letter. Such a principle is also generally accepted by most United States Catholic theologians and ethicists. It is not merely the bishops who strongly endorse the principle of discrimination. Some might be surprised by such strong support from the

United States for such a principle. The principle of discrimination has not been central in official universal Catholic hierarchical teaching on peace and war. In fact it has been maintained by some that official Catholic teaching does not explicitly recognize and use the principle of discrimination.[3] In addition, in contemporary moral theology Catholic revisionists propose a theory of proportionalism which maintains that the direct killing of noncombatants is a nonmoral evil which might be justified for a proportionate reason. A good number of Roman Catholic theologians in the United States espouse and use proportionalism in their moral methodology.

Why is there such support in the United States for the principle of discrimination? There is no easy answer to such a question, but a number of considerations might shed some light on this strong support.

Much writing and discussion about just war exist in the United States. Thanks to the significant efforts of the Protestant theologian Paul Ramsey, who died in the winter of 1988, great emphasis was given to the principle of discrimination.[4] Ramsey staunchly defended (probably wrongly) its historical foundation as far back as Augustine and its continuing validity and necessity today. Ramsey's significant work set the stage for much of the discussion by theological ethicists in the United States.

One of the objections frequently made against a just-war theory is that it so often serves only to accept and justify war and not to limit it. Would this moral theory ever be able to stand up and say No? Pacifists have often raised a similar question to just-war theorists.[5] As a result, then, Catholic just-war theorists in the United States were painfully conscious of the need to use the theory as a limit to the ravages of war. The more recent attempt to see pacifism and just war as somewhat complementary rather than totally opposed positions also helped support the importance of the principle of discrimination.[6]

In the broader context of the contemporary discussions about technology much talk exists about the need for a rational control of technology. The fear of technology getting out of control is great. The principle of discrimination is a clear way of putting moral and rational restraints on what is technologically possible and feasible.

In the United States there has also been a strong recognition of the legal basis for the principle of discrimination. American military commanders have been punished for the indiscriminate killing of noncombatants. With this understanding as part of our cultural ethos it is easier to accept the moral basis for the same principle of discrimination.

Perhaps too a sense of guilt is present about the fact that we Americans were the first and only nation to ever drop atomic bombs. At the time some Catholics questioned their use, but in general little or no moral outcry was made. Since then, many Catholic thinkers have judged the dropping of such bombs to have been morally wrong.

In the last few decades an increased emphasis on the right to life and on the human rights of all, especially the poor and the defenseless, has become evident. Noncombatants in war readily fit into that category. Also the United States bishops and many theologians have publicly called for an end to the death penalty.[7] Efforts by Cardinal Bernardin and others to propose a consistent ethic of life also strengthen and buttress the principle of discrimination with its prohibition of direct attacks on noncombatants.[8]

For these and other reasons it seems there has been firm support in the United States for the principle of discrimination. One example testifies to that support. An article in moral theology is not likely to become a classic which is frequently cited and used in the ensuing years and decades. However, such has been the case with John C. Ford's article upholding the principle of discrimination and condemning the allied obliteration bombing during the Second World War.[9] I would even be willing to claim that no other single article in recent Catholic moral theology has been cited or used more often than the Ford article.

In all the literature on the subject two generic types of grounds are proposed for rejecting the principle of discrimination, or noncombatant immunity. Some deny the principle of discrimination because of its incompatibility with an ethical theory such as utilitarianism. Others, especially those writing from a strategic perspective, deny the principle because of unacceptable conclusions about nuclear use and deterrence policies which are based on this principle.

In the course of the discussions among the participants at the two German–United States symposia on Catholic teaching on war and peace it became clear that many German participants did not accept as an absolute norm the principle of discrimination, or noncombatant immunity, because of the moral theory of proportionalism. This theory of proportionalism which is now favored by many German theologians maintains that for a proportionate reason one can do a nonmoral evil such as directly killing.

The traditional manuals of moral theology accept the basic principle that the direct killing of the innocent is always wrong. This principle according to the manuals is grounded deontologically. Such actions are intrinsically and always wrong. The consequences or circumstances cannot enter in to modify or change this basic principle. This principle of no direct killing of the innocent is then applied to other issues. Noncombatants are innocent, and therefore the direct killing of noncombatants is always and intrinsically evil. The norm of noncombatant immunity is a specification of the principle that the direct killing of the innocent is intrinsically and always wrong.

In the course of the discussion at the symposia it became clear that there are three possible positions — the acceptance of the norm of noncombatant immunity as a specification of the deontologically derived principle that direct killing of the innocent is always wrong; the denial of an absolute norm of noncombatant immunity based on a theory of proportionalism; and the acceptance of the norm of noncombatant immunity based on a proportionalist analysis.

It is necessary to show how one can employ a theory of proportionalism to justify the norm of noncombatant immunity, or what is also called the principle of discrimination.[10]

The general theory of proportionalism in contemporary Catholic moral theology should not be confused with the principle of proportionality in the just-war theory, although there are many similarities. According to the theory finite created goods cannot be absolutized. These goods are always in relationship with other goods. Life itself is a finite human good, and, consequently, life cannot be absolutized. The Catholic tradition has recognized this by admitting circumstances in which life can be taken. According to the theory of proportionalism these created finite goods are nonmoral goods. To go against such a good is a nonmoral evil. A nonmoral evil can be justified for a proportionate reason. Disagreements exist about the exact meaning of proportionality and about the understanding of what is the good to be attained, but in general the theory maintains that nonmoral evil can be justified for a proportionate reason.

Some norms by their very nature are formal norms, since the condemned action is described in moral terms. The Catholic theological tradition has always maintained that murder is wrong, but not all killing is wrong. Murder is a moral term, whereas killing is a physical or material term — the taking of a human life. Proportionalists maintain that the nonmoral evil of killing can be justified if there is a proportionate reason. In dealing with past norms that have existed within the Christian tradition proportionalists hold that these norms themselves were originally conceived on the basis of a proportionalist reasoning. There was no proportionate reason to justify such an act. Today proportionalists generally come to the conclusion that direct killing can be justified for a proportionate reason. However, on proportionalist grounds it might also be possible to defend the norm that direct killing is always wrong.

The following paragraphs will try to indicate the general lines of a proportionalist argument in favor of the norm of noncombatant immunity and at the same time propose a defense of some direct killing from a proportionalist understanding. Thus it will be clear that one can hold an absolute norm in practice, rejecting the direct killing of noncombatants while not necessarily accepting the principle, or the more general norm, that all direct killing is always wrong. Throughout this discussion direct is understood in accord with the manualistic understanding as that which is done or intended as an end in itself or as a means to an end.

A few years ago the philosophical literature often discussed the case of directly killing one person in order to save the lives of some others. This case was often discussed in terms of a military person about to execute twenty people but offering to let nineteen go free if you would be willing to shoot one of the twenty yourself. Is the direct killing of one proportionate to the end of saving the nineteen?[11] If one knows for sure that this is the only way of saving the nineteen and if the nineteen will definitely be saved, then I propose that direct killing in this case can be justified. The saving of nineteen lives justifies the direct killing of one, but there must be a moral certitude that the good effect will follow after the evil is done. Richard A. McCormick, who has developed proportionalism in greater depth than any other American moral theologian, maintains that the means is not proportionate to the good because the action goes against the associated good of freedom. Life and freedom are basic associated goods, and the means, in going against the associated basic good of human freedom, also undermines the good of human life. However, I think that McCormick too readily absolutizes the extortion which is involved in such a situation.[12] At times no other viable alternative might exist than to do the evil of one direct killing in order to save nineteen lives.

It should be pointed out that easier ways exist to defend the position that direct killing can sometimes be permitted for a proportionate reason. Think, for example, of the killing of the fetus in order to save the life of the mother. However, the case of directly killing one person in order to save nineteen others is proposed to show the difference between this case and the direct killing of noncombatants, or what is called the principle of discrimination.

The principle of discrimination can be defended on proportionalist grounds because there is not a proportionate reason to justify the direct killing of noncombatants. There are three important differences between this case and the case of directly killing one to save nineteen. First of all, the good effect in the first case of directly killing one to save nineteen can be clearly and accurately known and described. In the case of the indiscriminate killing of noncombatants the good to be achieved is not clear and cannot be accurately described. The good to be achieved might be the winning of the battle, the winning of the war, or the reduction in the ultimate number of lives lost. But by the very nature of the case this good cannot be accurately known or described with any great certainty.

Second, and most importantly, in the first case one knows with reasonable certitude that the good effect will be accomplished if the bad means is used. In the case of indiscriminate killing no certitude is present that the good effect will follow. It may or it may not follow. Many other factors have to enter into the situation in order that the good will be achieved. From a theoretical viewpoint this relationship of moral certitude between the evil done and the good achieved avoids the danger of a broad consequentialism based on the overall good to be achieved. In my analysis the evil of directly killing one is justified by the proportionate reason of saving the nineteen which will result from the action. The act itself is not disproportionate. (McCormick insists that there be a necessary connection between the evil done and the good achieved. From my perspective I think it is only necessary that one have reasonable certitude that the evil means will achieve the good effect.)

Third and finally, the danger of abuse is much more present in the case of the indiscriminate killing of noncombatants. The danger of abuse follows from the differences that exist between the two cases. The case of directly killing one in order to save nineteen is a very narrowly described reality and by definition would be very rare indeed. However, the situation of the indiscriminate killing of noncombatants cannot be described so narrowly. It takes many individual battles to win a war. The danger of self-deception is always great. The danger of the excessive use of force is omnipresent. Indiscriminate killing would not be merely an isolated instance as in the first case but would probably become the regular norm of acting.

One can make the case for the prohibition of the indiscriminate direct killing of noncombatants even on proportionalist grounds. By emphasizing the three aspects mentioned above one can conclude to a practically exceptionless moral norm of noncombatant immunity that also justifies the legal enactment and enforcement of noncombatant immunity. All the reasons mentioned earlier also bolster one's willingness to make such an argument. Thus, all in all we can understand why in the United States strong support for the principle of discrimination is evident.

Other Methodological Differences

From the viewpoint of theological methodology both documents recognize the presence of sin and insist on the already-but-not-yet aspect of Christian eschatology. However, the West German document seems to put a greater stress on the existence of human sinfulness and the difference between the now and the eschatological future.

Sin and its effects are mentioned in both letters. The West German document develops this at much greater length and depth in terms of the consequences for the state, thereby justifying the state's right to defend itself and its citizens. The Christian view includes "a sober and vigilant consideration of the treacherous and perfidious nature of evil in the world" (103). "For that reason the Church has always adhered to the necessity of protecting the innocent against brutality and oppression, combating injustice, and defending justice and righteousness" (104). "This protection is first and foremost the task of the government" (105). In an earlier passage the West German letter again recognizes that one of the foremost duties of a government's policies lies in protecting the legal order at home as well as safeguarding the existence and freedom of a nation against aggression and extortion from the outside (15). The Sermon on the Mount's injunction to resist not evil (Matt. 5:39) cannot be directly applied to the organization of social and political life. Such renunciation of force takes place at the expense of the well-being of others and of third parties. By resisting injustice and oppression, and by protecting the rights of the innocent, the state is the minister of God (45, 46). This letter recognizes some truth in the criticism of the heathen against some of the early Christians who had nothing to do with the state. These Christians benefited from the peace guaranteed by the state but did not help in bearing the corresponding burden (55). An ethic of responsibility calls for Christians to accept and aid the role of the state with its use of force.

In a similar fashion the West German letter puts more emphasis on the discontinuity between the present and the eschatological fullness. On two different occasions the German bishops warn against collapsing the eschaton by thinking that eternal peace can be present in this world as an historically obtainable program (75, 97). The peace of Christ in its complete form transcends the limits of historical feasibility. One must have the greatest skepticism about those doctrines of salvation which accept the development of humankind toward a condition of perfect humanity and peacefulness or which desire to bring about the future of an intact world by the use of revolutionary force (97). Such an eschatology also grounds the criticism of totalitarian regimes and provides the framework for a realistic ethic of responsibility which justifies the use of force by the state.

The more strictly ethical methodology in the West German letter also reinforces the realistic ethic of responsibility which is emphasized more in this document than in the American document. In its ethical methodology the German letter insists on a greater complexity by emphasizing the "and" more than the United States letter. The very title of the two documents illustrates this point. The United States letter is entitled "The Challenge of Peace: God's Promise and Our Response," whereas the West German bishops' letter is entitled "Out of Justice, Peace." Very frequently the West German letter brings together justice and peace. The very opening paragraph insists that justice creates peace (1). The biblical section insists on the complex nature of peace and frequently mentions justice. Such an understanding also sets the stage for the recognition that sometimes force and violence can be justified in the name of justice. Peace is not an absolute but is seen in relationship to many other realities such as freedom, justice, and security (24). The United States letter also sees peace as a complex reality, but a tendency is evident not to emphasize the complexity as much as the West German bishops do.

The realism of the West German letter is underscored by the insistence on "and" in developing a twofold mission with regard to peace — the promotion of peace and the maintenance of peace. Both approaches are necessary, but the just-defense approach fits in with the need to maintain the fragile peace that is existing (98ff). The complexity of the nature of peace and of the struggle for peace are recognized in both letters but more explicitly so in "Out of Justice, Peace."

Another important methodological concern in moral theology is the importance of historical consciousness with its emphasis on development and change without denying some continuity. Again, both documents recognize historical consciousness in their methodology, but the West German document gives a greater emphasis to it. In its discussion of the just-war theory the West German letter concentrates more on its historical development and accentuates the changes that have occurred even to the point of speaking now about just defense and not just war. The United States letter strongly insists on the universal norm derived from the principle of discrimination which is true in all circumstances. Such an emphasis is lacking in the German letter.

A very significant difference in the two letters concerns the level of the specificity of the moral judgments involved. From the very beginning the drafters of the United States document insisted on the need to be in dialogue with policymakers and the contemporary policy debate. For that reason all the drafts of the letter recognized the need to make many concrete prudential judgments. The insistence on the need for such specific concrete judgments raised in a very acute way the question of the teaching role and authority of the bishops. The final document recognizes the different levels of moral teachings found in the letter. At times the bishops reassert universally binding principles such as noncombatant immunity. At other times they reaffirm teachings of the pope and the Second Vatican Council. At other times they apply moral principles in particular cases. These specific moral judgments, while not binding in conscience, are to be given serious attention and consideration by Catholics as they determine whether their moral judgments are consistent with the gospel (9, 10). The German letter does not make nearly as many specific judgments as the United States letter. There is no doubt that the United States letter was quite influential precisely because it did make such judgments and entered into the policy debate at that level. At the same time such a methodology also underscores the recognition that the church is a community of moral discourse in which people united in the Christian faith dialogue and discuss the most significant questions facing humankind today.

The Drafting Process

Another important "methodological" difference concerns the process involved. The United States document was drafted by a committee of five bishops with very different perspectives on the issues involved. This committeee consulted widely with experts from all the relevant areas of competence involved and with representative spokespersons of all the spectrum of opinions involved. In addition three successive drafts were publicly distributed and discussed before the bishops voted on the final document. The West German letter went through three drafts proposed by a small team of experts who received comments from the bishops. The bishops' committee was in charge of the fourth draft, which the body of bishops discussed and released as their final document. There are advantages and disadvantages to both processes.

In my judgment the West German letter is much better in its consistency, coherence, and clarity. This is to be expected since the more closed and narrow drafting process should bring about a more coherent and unified document. Mention has already been made here of the methodological aspects which cohere with a realistic morality of responsibility recognizing the need and obligation of government to use force for self-defense in a sinful world.

On the other hand, consistency, coherence, and clarity are not outstanding characteristics of the United States letter. The argument in favor of self-defense and deterrence, as well as the clear rejection of unilateral nuclear disarmament, need to be developed in greater breadth and depth. The need to please drafters of different persuasions and the tensions involved in the inevitable compromises are bound to affect the consistency and coherence of a document. Lack of clarity is also more apparent in the United States document. To this day many commentators have misunderstood the United States bishops to say that all use of nuclear weapons is categorically prohibited. The intricate argument underlying the acceptability of some deterrence and its relationship to use was not even understood by the majority of the United States bishops themselves even after all their debate and discussions. At the final meeting in Chicago the bishops at first passed an amendment by Archbishop John Quinn: "Nevertheless, there must be no misunderstanding of our opposition on moral grounds to any use of nuclear weapons."[13] Such a resolution logically would put the bishops behind unilateral nuclear disarmament, for they firmly accepted the norm that a nation cannot threaten to do what it cannot morally do. Later, and only after strong urging by Cardinal Bernardin, the chair of the drafting committee, the bishops reversed themselves.

However, from an ecclesiological perspective the United States process is most significant. The bishops exercised their pastoral teaching function by listening and dialoguing in as broad a way as possible. No better model for the bishops could be followed in trying to discern the spirit and truth. This wide-ranging and public consideration and dialogue compare very favorably with the very private and narrow consultation involved in the writing of most previous church documents both on a national level and at the Vatican. The process itself becomes an important part of both the teaching and the learning process for all in the church. As a result of the process most bishops and many faithful had a greater sense of owning the final document.

Substantive Differences

Many significant differences exist between the two letters on the three important substantive or content questions of pacifism, the use of nuclear weapons, and nuclear deterrence.

Pacifism

The West German and United States bishops agree that individuals can be pacifists, but the state cannot embrace a pacifist position. However, the United States bishops are much stronger in their support of pacifism than are the German bishops. The West German document (91) cites the new consideration of the Second Vatican Council regarding nonviolence: "In the same spirit, we cannot but express our admiration for all who forego the use of violence to vindicate their rights and resort to those other means of defense which are available to weaker parties, provided it can be done without general harm to the rights and duties of others and of the community" (GS 78). The document also accepts the pacifism and conscientious objection of those who refuse to accept military service, but it recognizes some strain in their approach just as it recognizes a strain in the approach of those who are soldiers. If everyone were to follow the example of the pacifists and the conscientious objectors, it would "create a vacuum of power which can lead to vulnerability to political blackmail, something which they certainly wish to avoid" (201).

The United States bishops are stronger in their support of nonviolence and pacifism. The American bishops in a meeting in Rome in January 1983 had been cautioned about their position that nonviolence was a second tradition in the church alongside the just-war tradition.[14] However, the final document is strong in defense of a tradition of nonviolence and pacifism. "In the centuries between the fourth century and our own day, the theme of Christian nonviolence and Christian pacifism has echoed and re-echoed, sometimes more stongly, sometimes more faintly" (115). The bishops assert that both just war and nonviolence find their roots in the Christian theological tradition: both contribute to the full moral vision needed in pursuit of human peace. The two perspectives support and complement one another, each preserving the other from distortion (121). In their discussion on nonviolence and pacifism the United States bishops cite the Pastoral Constitution on the Church in the Modern World, giving praise "to those who renounce the use of violence in the vindication of their rights." However, "The Challenge of Peace" (118) omits the condition found in the very same sentence of the pastoral constitution — "provided this can be done without injury to the rights and duties of others or of the community itself." Thus, the United States document is much stronger than the West German document on the place of pacifism and nonviolence in the Christian tradition and at the present moment.

The Use of Nuclear Weapons

On the use of nuclear weapons, the United States bishops propose a three-level consideration. The first level expressly condemns total war and cites the famous sentence of the Pastoral Constitution on the Church in the Modern World: "Any act of war aimed indiscriminately at the destruction of entire cities or extensive areas along with their population is a crime against God and man itself. It merits unequivocal and unhesitating condemnation" (GS 80). However, the United States bishops understand this condemnation of total war in the light of the principle of discrimination and of noncombatant immunity. Counterpopulation warfare is wrong. No Christian can rightfully carry out orders or policies directly aimed at killing noncombatants (147-149).

On the second level, based on the principle of proportionality according to which the negative dangers and risks are too high, the letter comes out against the first use of nuclear weapons. Nonnuclear attacks by the enemy must be resisted by other than nuclear means (150-156). On a third level the question concerns the retaliatory (as distinguished from first use), counterforce (as distinguished from counterpopulation or countercity) use of nuclear weapons. The bishops do not absolutely condemn the possibility of a just use of retaliatory counterforce weapons, but the letter is highly skeptical about such use. The burden of proof remains on those who accept that meaningful limitation is possible (157-161).

It should be noted here that the position on nuclear use taken by the United States bishops is intimately connected with their position on deterrence. According to the American letter one cannot intend to do what one cannot actually do morally (178). Deterrence involves the moral intention to do what is threatened. If there is no possible legitimate use of nuclear weapons, then there is no morally acceptable possibility of nuclear deterrence. By not absolutely condemning retaliatory counterforce use, the bishops leave open the door to justify a counterforce deterrent.

Some objections have been raised from various perspectives to the position of the United States bishops on the use of nuclear weapons. First, is the failure to condemn all use consistent with their condemnation of first use and their condemnation of the concept of fighting and winning a limited nuclear war? Second, is the first use of limited nuclear weapons always wrong? Third, does deterrence necessarily involve the moral intention to use the deterrent? Fourth, on the basis of a centimeter of ambiguity about a retaliatory counterforce use of nuclear weapons, can one legitimately accept as much counterforce deterrence as the bishops seem to justify?

The position of the German bishops on the use of nuclear weapons is less developed. The West German letter accepts the condemnation of total war found in the Pastoral Constitution on the Church in the Modern World of Vatican II. It does not condemn the first use of counterforce nuclear weapons. The West German bishops maintain that any use of nuclear weapons must be judged in the light of the principle of proportionality. The main criticism to be voiced about the position of the West German bishops is the need to spell out more clearly what is the paticular position on use. Again note that the West German bishops do not use or apparently even accept the principle of discrimination, or noncombatant immunity.

Deterrence

Many areas of agreement exist between the two letters on the question of deterrence. There is a limited moral acceptance or toleration of deterrence but with strict conditions attached. Also, both admit that in the long run deterrence is not a reliable means for preventing war.

The West German document maintains that the goal of nuclear deterrence is the prevention of war. "The intention of preventing war with all one's strength must become credible by virtue of the choice of the whole range of arms. The methods chosen to pursue one's security policy should be measured in terms of the goal of preventing war" (143). The use of a threat of mass destruction, which one must never carry out, is effective and morally acceptable if the whole range of security policy is directed toward the goal of preventing war and if the military measures remain integrated within the higher ranking concept of maintaining peace by political means (146).

Since the United States bishops accept the principle that you cannot intend to do what you cannot morally do, the principle of discrimination and the principle of proportion govern which weapons and which targeting policy can be used as a threat. Also, some targeting of military targets might also be wrong by reason of the disproportionate evil involved. The United States bishops thus propose strictly conditioned moral acceptance of some limited counterforce deterrence (178ff).

The differences are obvious. The primary ethical difference remains the question: Do deterrence and its threat involve a moral intention to use? The West German letter says No by its recognition that the use of a threat of mass destruction, which one must never morally carry out, is particularly effective in preventing war and can be morally acceptable within a policy aimed at preventing war (146). The United States letter says Yes. The existence and role of the principle of discrimination also remain strong points of divergence.

In the course of the discussions at the two German–United States symposia on the Catholic teaching on peace and war it became evident that many differences exist over the positions taken on deterrence and the moral justification of deterrence. However, in my judgment two things in common stand out among all the participants and also between the two pastoral letters. First, all the participants were opposed to unilateral nuclear disarmament. Some today would argue for unilateral nuclear disarmament, but neither of the two letters nor any of the participants in these symposia held such a position. The second thing in common involves a matter of judgment. In my judgment the weakest part in all the positions proposed is the defense of deterrence. There seems to be no argument or reason proposed for nuclear deterrence that does not have some problematic aspect about it. In the course of the discussion many seemed to agree with this judgment. But now it is incumbent upon me to give the reasons for my judgment that in all the approaches the defense of some nuclear deterrence remains somewhat weak and open to questioning. Four different positions that emerged in the discussions will be analyzed and criticized.

The first position is taken in the United States letter. As already pointed out, the United States bishops see an intimate connection between the use of nuclear weapons and deterrence by nuclear weapons. One cannot intend to do what one cannot do morally. For a nation the threat in deterrence involves the intention to use. Therefore a nation can only threaten in deterrence what it can morally use. If the United States bishops had opposed all use of nuclear weapons, they would have to oppose all nuclear deterrence. The United States letter, as mentioned, opposes all countercity or counterpopulation use of nuclear weapons and the first use of nuclear weapons but does not absolutely condemn the use of retaliatory counterforce nuclear weapons. Since the United States bishops do not condemn all use, they can justify some deterrence based on counterforce weapons to be used in retaliation after one has already been attacked by nuclear weapons.

Two possible objections can be raised to this position. First, it seems that the very logic of the argument, which comes to the conclusion that countercity as well as first use of nuclear weapons is wrong, should also come to the conclusion that all use of nuclear weapons is wrong. As already mentioned, at the final discussion of the document the United States bishops did adopt an amendment opposing any use of nuclear weapons.[15] However, the bishops quickly reversed themselves. Such an amendment would have unravelled the intricate reasoning of the letter and logically would have taken away from the document the moral justification of deterrence. However, the episode confirms my judgment that the logic in the bishops' letter goes against all use of nuclear weapons. It was the need to justify some deterrence that seems to be the basis for leaving the door slightly ajar on the retaliatory counterforce use of nuclear weapons.

Second, from the viewpoint of deterrence itself the basic question is the amount or level of deterrence which can be justified on the basis of the position of the United States bishops. Some would maintain that counterpopulation deterrence is necessary to achieve the purpose of deterrence, but this cannot be accepted by the United States bishops. My question about the level or amount of deterrence comes from a different perspective. On the basis of merely leaving the door slightly ajar on retaliatory counterforce use, it seems that the bishops try to justify quite a bit of deterrence.

A second position denies the absoluteness of the principle of discrimination, or the norm of noncombatant immunity, and does not consider all countercity or counterpopulation use or deterrence to be morally wrong. This position was held by participants from both the German and the United States groups at the symposia. Such an approach can accept as legitimate some counterpopulation deterrence.

Such a position is able to accept the morality of counterpopulation and countercity deterrence, yet at the great cost of denying the exceptionless norm of noncombatant immunity. At the very minimum this norm has been accepted legally and has served as an important limit to the ravages of war in the contemporary period. The position denying the norm of noncombatant immunity would place fewer moral constraints on both nuclear use and deterrence.

A third position separates the order of deterrence from the order of use. Deterrence is one moral reality; use is another. The justification of deterrence is the intention to prevent war at all costs. This intention allows for the amount of deterrence which is necessary to prevent war and basically makes no distinction between counterforce and countercity deterrence. If deterrence fails, then the question of use is an entirely different question which must be faced on its own grounds.

The primary weakness of this position is the ethical understanding of the relationship between the order of deterrence

;

and the order of use. To make the threat real at least someone in the chain of command would have to have the moral
intention to use the weapons. From a moral perspective it
does not seem that the order of deterrence and the order of
use can be separated so much. Likewise, in practice it would
seem that if one was threatening to use the weapons, then
in the time of need one would as a matter of fact use the
weapons.

A fourth position also emerged in the course of the discussions but was not spelled out as precisely as the others. To
threaten any nuclear attack against another nation is wrong,
but no other viable option exists at the present time. Such
a threat is justified provided efforts are being made to elimi-
nate the need for such threats.

Such a position certainly appreciates the dilemma of nuclear
deterrence, but it seems to lack any deep theological or philosophical basis. From my own perspective it might be that
one could develop such an understanding in the light of a
theology of compromise. The theology of compromise recognizes that the presence of sin in the world will at times force
people to do things which under ordinary circumstances they
would not do. Precisely because sin is present in the world,
one has an obligation to try to overcome that sinful situation
which necessitates our doing a particular action. However,
this theory would then have to grapple with the question of
the limits which can be tolerated in such sinful situations. Can
one accept or do *any* evil provided one is trying to overcome
the evil situation? At the very minimum this position calls
for a more developed theoretical analysis and justification.

In conclusion, at these particular meetings all agreed on
the need for some deterrence at the present time, but in my
judgment problematic aspects are present in all the positions
proposed in defense of deterrence. The dilemma of nuclear
deterrence continues to exist both in theory and in practice.

This chapter has attempted to analyze from the perspective of moral theology the differences, both methodological
and substantive, between the West German and the United
States pastoral letters on peace and the nuclear question. In
the process some questions have been raised to both letters

to facilitate the ongoing discussion. In conclusion one can only point out the fascinating questions posed for Catholic ecclesiology by the differences of these two letters in the areas of ethical methodology, moral principles, and specific positions on nuclear use and deterrence.

NOTES

1. An English translation of the West German pastoral letter can be found in James V. Schall, ed., *Out of Justice, Peace: Joint Pastoral Letter of the West German Bishops; Winning the Peace: Joint Pastoral Letter of the French Bishops* (San Francisco, CA: Ignatius Press, 1984). References in the text will be to the paragraph numbers of the West German letter as found in this translation.

2. National Conference of Catholic Bishops, *The Challenge of Peace: God's Promise and Our Response* (Washington, DC: United States Catholic Conference, 1983). References in the text will be to the paragraph numbers of this document, which has also been republished in a number of places.

3. Brian V. Johnstone, "Noncombatant Immunity: The Origins of the Principle in Theology and Law," *Studia Moralia* 24 (1986): 115-148, especially 132ff. It should be noted that Johnstone himself fully supports the principle of discrimination.

4. Paul Ramsey, *War and the Christian Conscience: How Shall Modern War Be Conducted Justly?* (Durham, NC: Duke University Press, 1961); Paul Ramsey, *The Just War: Force and Political Responsibility* (New York, NY: Charles Scribner's Sons, 1968).

5. John Howard Yoder, *When War is Unjust: Being Honest in Just-War Thinking* (Minneapolis, MN: Augsburg Publishing House, 1984).

6. James F. Childress, "Just-War Criteria," in Thomas A. Shannon, ed., *War or Peace? The Search for New Answers* (Maryknoll, NY: Orbis Press, 1980), pp. 40-58. The United States bishops accept such a complementary approach in their pastoral letter (74).

7. Franz Böckle and Jacques Pohier, eds., *The Death Penalty and Torture*, Concilium: Religion in the Seventies, 120 (New York: Seabury, 1979).

8. Cardinal Joseph Bernardin, "Toward a Consistent Ethic of Life," *Origins* 13 (1983-84): 491-494; "Enlarging the Dialogue on the Consistent Ethic of Life," *Origins* 13 (1983-84): 705-709; "Consistent Ethic of Life and the Abortion Issue," *Origins* 14 (1984-85):

120-122; "Religion and Politics: The Future Agenda," *Origins* 14 (1984-85): 321-323, 328.

9. John C. Ford, "The Morality of Obliteration Bombing," *Theological Studies* 5 (1944): 261-309.

10. Some principles are more specific than others. The principle of no direct killing of the innocent is more general than the principle of discrimination. To bring out this difference I occasionally refer to the principle of no direct killing of the innocent and the norm of noncombatant immunity. However, it would also be correct to refer to both as norms and not as principles.

11. Bernard Williams in J. J. C. Smart and Bernard Williams, *Utilitarianism: For and Against* (Cambridge: Cambridge University Press, 1973), pp. 98, 99.

12. Richard A. McCormick, "A Commentary on the Commentaries," in Richard A. McCormick and Paul Ramsey, eds., *Doing Evil to Achieve Good: Moral Choice in Conflict Situations* (Chicago, IL: Loyola University Press, 1978), pp. 193-267.

13. Jim Castelli, *The Bishops and the Bomb: Waging Peace in a Nuclear Age* (Garden City, NY: Doubleday Image Books, 1983), p. 169.

14. "Rome Consultation on Peace and Disarmament: A Vatican Synthesis," *Origins* 12 (1982-83): 694.

15. Castelli, *The Bishops and the Bomb*, p. 169.

9: Official Catholic Social Teaching and Conscience

This study will explore how the social teaching of the universal church and the recent pastoral letters proposed by the United States bishops treat some aspects of conscience. Conscience will be understood in the classical sense as the judgment about the morality of an action to be done or omitted and will be limited to antecedent conscience. Obviously social teaching or social ethics in general does not directly and systematically discuss the nature or the function of conscience, for such a treatment belongs to general moral theology. However, the social teaching of the church cannot ignore the reality of conscience, which plays so central a role in the moral life.

From within the Catholic perspective perhaps the most characteristic and distinctive aspect of the understanding of conscience in Catholic social teaching is the recognition of the freedom of the conscience of the individual Christian and the diversity of concrete judgments which can exist on social matters within the church. While recognizing such freedom and diversity, the social teachings try to influence the formation of conscience. In addition, church social teaching does give some indication of how the judgments of conscience are made, even though there is no systematic or in-depth development of how individual consciences make concrete judgments and decisions. Official universal Catholic social teaching and the more recent social teaching proposed by the United States bishops will be examined for what they say about these two aspects of conscience.

Universal Social Teaching

Official universal Catholic social teaching is generally associated with the papal encyclicals beginning with Pope Leo XIII's *Rerum Novarum* of 1891 and including conciliar and other documents of the universal church down to the present. Although at first sight it may seem surprising, the most significant aspect of the understanding of conscience mentioned in this teaching is the freedom of conscience and the possibility of pluralism and diversity within the Catholic Church on specific questions of social morality. This position has consistently been upheld in the tradition, and there is no appreciative development in the statement of the position, even though, as will be pointed out in the next section, there seems to have been development in the reasons behind the position. This thesis will be proved by examining the documents themselves, by the testimony of the commentators on these documents, by pointing out in reality the pluralism and diversity that have existed in the area of social morality within the church, and finally by proposing the reasons why such a freedom and range of diversity must exist within the Catholic Church.

The documents forming the tradition explicitly recognize the legitimate freedom of conscience and the possibility of diversity within the church on specific judgments in the social realm. An excellent illustration of this position has been the attitude of the tradition on the best form of government. Traditionally church documents have been reluctant to claim that there can be only one form of government and all other forms are morally bad. The documents have generally stressed the principles of justice that should be present within any political society no matter what its particular form — e.g., monarchy, democracy, or even dictatorship. Over the centuries the church has existed with all different forms of political government and has been hesitant to condemn a particular form. There are indications, especially in the last forty years, that the official teaching is more open to democratic forms of government, but it is interesting that one-person rule or one-party rule has never been condemned as such. The Pastoral Constitution on the Church in the Modern World of Vatican Council II explicitly states that the church "is bound to no particular form of human culture, nor to any political, economic, or social system."[1]

The official documents of the universal church both insist on and indicate the duty and right of the church to teach authoritatively on moral aspects of the political, social, and economic orders, but at the same time these documents also recognize the limits of the church's authoritative teaching in these areas. In explaining and praising what his predecessor, Leo XIII, had done, Pope Pius XI in his encyclical *Quadragesimo Anno* in 1931 characterized Leo as relying solely on the unchangeable principles drawn from right reason and divine revelation.[2] In his encyclical on atheistic communism the same Pius XI described the function of the teaching church as proposing the guiding principles which are susceptible of varied concrete applications according to the diversified conditions of times, places, and peoples.[3] Both the competency and the limits of the church intervention in the social order are determined by the unchanging moral principles derived from the natural law and revelation. Pope John XXIII in *Mater et Magistra* made the same distinction between norms or principles and their application. In applying these principles the pope recognized that even sincere Catholics may have differing positions.[4] More recent documents also maintain the diversity of specific judgments and actions within the church. *Octogesima Adveniens*, the 1971 letter of Pope Paul VI, explicitly recognizes that it is neither the pope's ambition nor his mission to put forward solutions which have universal validity.[5] Thus the documents themselves, both in what they actually propose and in what they explicitly say about what they propose, give great freedom to the individual Christian in concrete decisions in the social realm.

The commentators on the papal teaching have universally recognized that official church teaching allows for a pluralism of specific decisions and approaches. Calvez and Perrin are typical of the pre-Vatican II commentators in describing the roles of authoritative church teaching and of the conscience of the believer in terms of unchangeable principles and changing applications. The church teaching defends and promotes values which are unchangeable. The competency of church teaching extends to essential determinations of the natural law and the fundamental conditions of action conformable to the law of charity. Beyond this realm of unchangeable natural law the church recognizes the freedom of all in the realm of application precisely because of the changing circumstances involved.[6] Post-Vatican II commentators recognize that the solutions to particular problems can only be proposed on the basis of a discernment done on the local level.[7]

The life of the Catholic Church well illustrates the diversity and pluralism of approaches in the areas of political, social, and economic institutions. As already noted, the church has existed with and continues to exist with many different types of social structures and institutions. The difference between unchanging principles and changing applications, which was heavily emphasized in the pre-Vatican II times, is well illustrated in the principle of subsidiarity and its applications. According to this principle the state should encourage individuals, families, and other lesser associations and groups to do what they can and should do within society, while the state should intervene only when no other institution in society can effectively deal with the issue. This principle has been interpreted differently by different people. Catholics in most of the Western world have often differed over what is the proper role of the state. In the United States both democratic and republican proposals, both liberal and conservative approaches, have appealed to the principle of subsidiarity.[8] Within the Catholic community in the United States there have been what can accurately be called conservative, reforming, and even radical approaches to the social order, but all claiming to be based on Catholic social teaching.[9] Thus the Catholic reality bears out the diversity and pluralism which can exist within the context of official Catholic social teaching. While insisting on the legitimacy of authoritative church teaching to guide the social realm, the church has also insisted on the limits of its teaching and thereby recognized and protected the freedom of the individual church member in making concrete judgments and decisions in the social order.

What are the ultimate reasons why the church recognizes a diversity of specific judgments, decisions, and actions in the social realm within the parameters of its general moral teaching? Ecclesiological, theological, and epistemological reasons all support the theory and practice of the church in recognizing a pluralism of such concrete judgments and actions in the social realm. From an ecclesiological perspective the church claims a universal mission to all people and all times and in all historical and cultural circumstances. As a result the church cannot ally itself to just one political or economic system. The universality of the church demands an openness to all approaches, while insisting that all social structures and institutions work toward greater justice. Naturally limits exist on what the church can and should accept, but its universal mission argues for a great latitude in structuring the social, political, and economic orders.

From a contemporary theological perspective the gospel must have something to say about human existence in the social order. However, faith and the gospel must always be mediated through the human and especially through the data of all the human sciences involved and through all the relevant facts. The gospel and faith do not provide a substitute for or a way around all the complexities of the human. Some would argue that the church has no competence to teach on social questions primarily because the church cannot claim to have expertise in this area. It is true that the competence of the church is based on the gospel, but the gospel must become incarnated in particular situations, institutions, and choices, Gospel values must influence particular facts and judgments. However, the gospel is mediated through the human, and in the midst of human complexity one must recognize that it is impossible to claim that there is only one possible Christian approach.

This theological outlook based on how faith and the gospel must always be mediated through the human is intimately connected with the epistemological reason for recognizing the possibility of pluralism and diversity on specific decisions, structures, actions, and judgments. The more specific and complex the reality, the less the possibility of certitude. The principle of logic maintains that the possibility of certitude decreases as specificity and complexity increase. On the level of the general and the formal one can have a great degree of certitude: for example, injustice or murder is always wrong. But whether or not the particular action involves injustice is a much more complex matter, and often a legitimate diversity of opinion is present. Ecclesiological, theological, and epistemological reasons support the position that within the social realm the church must recognize the possibility of diversity and pluralism on specific judgments and hence recognize and protect the legitimate freedom of the believer in these areas.

The second important aspect of conscience considered in the traditional Catholic social teaching is the generic understanding of how individual conscience functions. Church teaching in the social realm has the purpose of forming the conscience of believers while at the same time safeguarding a legitimate freedom of conscience. One should not expect within social teaching an explicit, systematic, in-depth, theoretical development of how conscience works, but the documents must be working with some implicit understanding of how conscience does function and how the individual makes decisions. The primary purpose of the social teaching is to form the consciences of the individual Christians, so that the documents must reveal some concept of how conscience works and operates.

In the developing tradition of Catholic social teaching some change seems evident in the understanding of how conscience operates. This change can best be understood in the context of the shift from classicism to historical consciousness. Chapter five above described the shift to historical consciousness, and the present consideration will develop the understanding of conscience in the light of this move toward greater historical consciousness. Classicism moves from the abstract and the general to the particular and the concrete, emphasizes the immutable natural-law principles, and tends to be more deductive. Historical mindedness does not begin with the abstract and the general but rather with the particular and the concrete, emphasizes the changing character of history, and tends to be somewhat more inductive in its approach. Without doubt the documents in the tradition do recognize such a change, although Paul VI is much stronger on historical consciousness than his successor John Paul II.[10]

The language of the earlier documents and the language of the earlier commentators emphasize the unchangeable principles and the changing applications. Natural law is understood as the unchanging given which is then applied to particular circumstances. The function of the individual conscience is to apply the principles to the changing situation. This classicist understanding of conscience coincides well with the manualistic understanding that conscience at least implicitly follows the method of the syllogism in arriving at its particular conclusions. However, in *Mater et Magistra* conscience is described in a way that does not necessarily have to be understood in a totally classicist vein. Here Pope John XXIII adopts the approach of Catholic Action to the functioning of conscience. The Catholic Action movement, spearheaded especially by Joseph Cardijn, proposed the famous three steps of see, judge, act. This approach by its very nature can break away somewhat from the abstract and totally deductive approach of a classicist understanding of conscience. Pope John XXIII still understands this threefold approach, however, as adapting the traditional norms to the circumstances of time and place.[11]

However, beginning with John XXIII one can note incipient changes in the development of historical consciousness. A major part of *Mater et Magistra* called for a reconstruction of the social relationships in truth, justice, and love.[12] Two years later Pope John XXIII in *Pacem in Terris* added an important element to this trinity — truth, justice, love, and freedom.[13] *Pacem in Terris* ends each of the four major parts of the encyclical with a description of the signs of the times. The Pastoral Constitution on the Church in the Modern World in its discussion of five subjects or issues of concern in the second part of the document begins each one of these chapters with a discussion of the signs of the times. Present is a definite switch from beginning with the abstract to beginning with the concrete, from an emphasis on the unchanging to an emphasis on the historical.

Without a doubt *Octogesima Adveniens*, the 1971 letter of Pope
Paul VI to Cardinal Roy, is the best illustration of historical
consciousness found in the documents of the tradition of the
social teaching of the Catholic Church. *Octogesima Adveniens*
begins by recognizing the diversity of situations facing the
contemporary world. In the midst of such widely varying
situations the pope insists it is neither his mission nor his ambition to propose a unified message or to put forward a solution which possesses universal validity. The local Christian
communities themselves in the light of their situation, the
gospel, and the social teaching of the church must come up
with their own solutions to these questions (par. 4).

The emphasis on history and historical change contrasts
with the approach taken in the earlier documents. Other documents did recognize changes which had occurred since the
previous pope had spoken on the subject, but the insistence
on change and new developments in *Octogesima Adveniens* stands
out. Pope Paul VI speaks about very rapid and profound
changes and points out special problems in the areas of
urbanization, youth, women, workers, victims of change,
discrimination, emigrant workers, the need to create employment, the media of social communication, and the environ-
ment (par. 8-22).

The older emphasis on the immutable and the unchanging is gone. In the midst of these rapid and profound changes
the human person discovers one's self anew and questions
one's self about the meaning of personal existence and collective survival (par. 7). This letter does not deny permanent
and eternal truths, but one cannot easily deduce from these
how one should act.

Octogesima Adveniens describes the church's social teaching
in a very historically conscious way. With all its dynamism
the social teaching of the church accompanies human beings
in their search for answers to the urgent problems of today.
The dynamic nature of the social teaching is spelled out by
describing it as drawing on the rich experiences of the past,
continuing its permanent preoccupations, and undertaking
the daring and creative innovations which the present state
of the world requires (par. 42).

The letter ends with a call to action and insists that amid

the diversity of situations, functions, and organizations each person must discern in one's conscience the actions that he or she is called to share in (par. 49). In the description of how conscience functions this letter avoids the description of conscience as applying abstract and immutable principles to concrete situations. The word used to describe the function of conscience is discernment — not the application of principles to concrete cases (par. 35ff). The pope appeals to utopias — the first such appeal in the history of the tradition of the social teaching of the church. Utopias are not abstract and immutable principles. Utopias as criticisms of existing societies provoke the forward-looking imagination to perceive in the present the disregarded possibilities hidden within it and to direct itself toward a fresh future. Utopias sustain social dynamism by appealing to the inventive powers of the human heart and mind. The Spirit dwelling within the Christian urges the believer to go beyond the limits and restrictions of every system and every ideology. This emphasis on conscience as discernment and the role of utopias recognizes that at the heart of the world dwells the mystery of the human person discovering the self as God's child in the course of an historical and psychological process wherein constraint and freedom as well as the weight of sin and the breath of the Spirit alternate and struggle for the upper hand (par. 37).

The description of conscience in *Octogesima Adveniens* differs markedly from the earlier emphasis on the application of immutable and absolute principles to changing circumstances. One cannot expect this document to give a detailed and systematic treatise on the nature and function of conscience, but the more historically conscious, concrete, and inductive characteristics of conscience are clearly present in the description of conscience as well as in the employment of the concepts of discernment and utopias.

Social Teaching of the United States Bishops

The first part of this study has examined the social teaching of the universal church to see what is said about the legitimate freedom of the conscience of the believer in social matters and what is said about the nature and function of conscience. The second part will examine the social teaching of the United States bishops, especially the last two recent pastoral letters on peace and the economy, to see how they treat the legitimate freedom of the conscience of members of the church and how they understand the role and function of conscience.[14]

The most characteristic aspect of the two United States pastoral letters is the greater specificity found in them and the more particular judgments made there in comparison to the documents of the universal hierarchical teaching office. The United States documents do not go against the teachings of the universal hierarchical magisterium, but they go beyond the universal documents in the sense of being much more specific. The pastoral letter on peace and nuclear war, for example, makes the judgment that the first use of even the smallest nuclear weapons is wrong.[15]

How do the United States documents look at the legitimate freedom of the conscience of the individual Catholic? By being more specific it would seem that these documents might actually give a lesser role to the freedom of the individual Catholic in social matters.

The two recent pastoral letters of the United States bishops were not written in a vacuum. The United States bishops had been speaking out on social issues in a more specific way for quite some time, and this became even more pronounced after the Second Vatican Council.[16] The impetus for such an approach also came from the acute social problems that were being faced in the United States during this time. Without doubt the national debate over the Vietnam War put pressure on the bishops to make some specific judgments about that war. Particular judgments were also made on many other current social problems facing the United States. Some debate has been present among Catholics in the United States about the widsom of the bishops making such specific and concrete judgments, but this has been the accepted approach of the bishops themselves.[17] From the very beginning many Catholics recognized that the pastoral letter on peace and the nuclear question would make such specific moral judgments.[18]

The ramifications of some of the specific judgments made in the first drafts of the pastoral letter on peace and the nuclear issue created attention. An informal consultation was held at the Vatican in January 1983 involving representatives of the United States bishops' conference with representatives of many Western European bishops' conferences and the Curia (Cardinal Ratzinger presided at the meeting) to discuss questions arising from the second draft of the pastoral letter. A summary of the meeting was prepared by Archbishop Roach and Cardinal Bernardin on January 25 and shared with the committee writing the pastoral letter. A longer memorandum written by Father Jan Schotte, secretary of the Pontifical Commission on Justice and Peace, summarized the meeting in greater detail. These two memoranda were sent to all the United States bishops with a covering memorandum by Archbishop Roach and Cardinal Bernardin on March 21, 1983.[19] The covering memorandum said that perhaps the crucial point of the exchanges was "to focus attention on the need to distinguish clearly between moral principles and their application to concrete realities — that is, between principles on the one hand and, on the other, specific applications of these principles via the assessment of factual circumstances." This distinction is necessary to avoid attaching an unwarranted level of authority to prudential, contingent judgments in which the complexity of the facts makes possible a number of legitimate options.[20]

The longer Schotte memorandum maintained that a clear line must be drawn between a statement of principle and practical choices based on prudential judgment. The need for this differentiation comes from the need to distinguish very clearly the different levels of teaching authority in the letter. This distinction will respect the freedom of the Christian as to what is binding and what is not binding and will safeguard the integrity of the faith so that nothing is proposed as the doctrine of the church which merely pertains to prudential judgments.[21]

The third draft of the pastoral letter on peace issued shortly thereafter and the final document approved in the next month clearly make this distinction. In the very beginning the final version of the peace pastoral distinguishes different levels of ethical discourse with correspondingly different levels of teaching authority. Universal moral principles and quotations from universal church teaching involve the teaching authority of bishops as such. However, at times the pastoral letter applies moral principles to specific cases which involve prudential judgments that can be interpreted differently by people of good will. The bishops themselves give as an example here their judgment about no first use of nuclear weapons. These judgments made in specific cases are not binding in conscience, but they should be given serious attention and consideration by Catholics. On the level of the application of principles a legitimate diversity and pluralism within the Catholic Church can exist.[22]

The pastoral letter on the economy continues in the same general direction. The letter maintains that in teaching the fundamentals of Christian faith, church teaching, and basic moral principles the bishops are proposing norms which should inform the consciences of the members of the church. On the other hand, the recommendations about specific policies for decisions in the economic sphere involve prudential judgments, and different conclusions are possible even among those who share the same moral principles and objectives.[23] Thus, even though the United States pastoral letters do make specific policy recommendations, they safeguard the legitimate freedom of the believer's conscience on specific, complex issues and policies.

The second question to be investigated concerns the understanding in the pastoral letters of the United States bishops of how conscience operates. As mentioned above, the January 1983 Vatican meeting insisted on the need to distinguish the various levels of moral teaching with the correspondingly different levels of authoritative teaching and described these levels primarily in terms of universal principles and the applications of these principles in particular historical circumstances. "The Challenge of Peace: God's Promise and Our Response" likewise uses the terminology of universal principles and their application to point out that on the level of application there can be a legitimate diversity within the church. The economic pastoral distinguishes the various levels of moral teaching, moves from principles to policies, but shies away from describing its practical judgments as applications of principles in discussing the different levels of its teaching.[24] There seems to be some change here.

The pastoral letter on peace claims to be following the methodology and the teaching of *Gaudium et Spes,* the Pastoral Constitution on the Church in the Modern World of Vatican II. The pastoral thus begins with a recognition of the signs of the time, especially in terms of the threat of nuclear destruction of the world. However, in general the structure of the document goes from the more general to the more specific. A scriptural understanding of peace is followed by a theological approach to the relationship between the kingdom of God and history. Then the document discusses the just-war criteria and nonviolence. The judgments about nuclear weapons and nuclear deterrence in the second chapter are made in light of the just-war principles of discrimination and proportionality in governing the way in which war is to be waged. The impression is given that these principles are applied to the present situation to arrive at the specific judgments made in the letter.

Is it legitimate, then, to conclude that the pastoral letter on peace understands the function of conscience as moving from the abstract and general to the particular and concrete, and proceeds by way of applying universal principles to specific circumstances? Although the document definitely gives the impression that it understands conscience to function in this way, the case can be made that as a matter of fact in the letter itself specific judgments of conscience are not necessarily the result of the application of universals to specific circumstances and are not based on a process of going from the abstract and the general to the particular and the concrete.

In my perspective a very specific judgment has influenced many of the other specific judgments and even affected some of the principles proposed in the pastoral letter on peace. This important judgment apparently was not and could not be made by the application of a general principle to particular circumstances. Unfortunately, the final version of the letter itself does not explain this particular judgment in great detail, nor does it explicitly recognize how important this judgment is in the overall development and structure of the pastoral letter. However, the case can be made to prove the centrality of this judgment and its influence on many of the other judgments and even on some of the theoretical principles proposed in the pastoral letter itself. I refer to the judgment, or conscience decision, not to demand total unilateral nuclear disarmament at this time. In reality this judgment is much more central in the pastoral letter than appears on the surface. In the course of the development of the document through its various drafts this judgment, or conscience decision, remains constant, while other changes on a more theoretical and general level were made to accommodate the continued conclusion about not demanding total unilateral nuclear disarmament at this time. The historical development of the document thus indicates the importance and centrality of the existential judgment about no unilateral disarmament.

If one makes the judgment that there should not be immediate and total unilateral nuclear disarmament at this time, then one must have reasons to justify the morality of nuclear deterrence at the present time. The history of the drafts indicates a continuing search for such a rationale that is needed to shore up this very significant existential judgment. The changing rationale proposed indicates that the nonnegotiable aspect throughout the development of the letter was the particular judgment itself and not the rationale which was proposed for it.

In the first draft of the letter the bishops developed a two-tiered approach to deterrence. Through five different steps they build up the justification for a barely justified deterrent. Here the draft accepts the principle that one cannot threaten to do what one cannot do. Since it is wrong to attack cities and civilian targets, it is wrong to threaten to attack them as part of a strategy of deterrence. The draft does not categorically condemn the use of nuclear weapons in response to the first use of nuclear weapons by others if these retaliatory weapons are restricted to military targets. This position is the basis for a barely justified nuclear deterrent involving counterforce nuclear weapons. However, the draft goes further by being willing to tolerate as a lesser evil what is understood to be the present United States deterrence policy involving counterpopulation deterrence. This type of deterrence can be tolerated as long as there are hopes that such deterrence will be a step toward the reduction of nuclear arms.[25]

The second draft drops the two-tiered consideration of deterrence. The document recognizes the moral and political paradox of deterrence, which by threatening the use of nuclear weapons has actually seemed to many to have prevented their use. The draft understands United States policy as directed against targets of value which either include civilian populations directly or involving killing large numbers of civilians in an indirect manner. The draft then tolerates this deterrence provided steps are being taken to reduce the overall nuclear strength and eventually to phase out nuclear deterrence and the threat of mutual assured destruction. The second draft sees this toleration as another way of expressing what Pope John Paul II said to the United Nations in June 1982: "In current conditions deterrence based on balance, certainly not as an end in itself, but as a step on the way toward a progressive disarmament may still be judged morally acceptable." There are limits and conditions on nuclear deterrence, but the draft does not call for unilateral nuclear disarmament.[26]

As time went on, the drafters became aware of a problem in their ethics. One cannot tolerate one's own intention to do evil. You can tolerate what some call nonmoral evil, but you can never tolerate your own intention to do moral evil. By the time of the third draft the committee also had in its possession a document from William Clark, the National Security Advisor, stating that "the United States does not target the Soviet civilian population as such." In the light of these developing understandings the third draft and the final version pose their position on deterrence. To prevent nuclear war from ever occurring and to protect and preserve the key moral values of justice, freedom, and independence, a conditional, limited acceptance of some counterforce deterrence is acceptable at the present time. A major condition is the need to see deterrence not as something permanent but as a step on the way to progressive disarmament. Many limits are proposed, but above all such deterrence must be limited to counterforce deterrence and not countercity or counterpopulation deterrence. Other conditions and limits are also expounded.[27]

A fascinating development occurred when the bishops voted on the final document in May 1983. The proposed document condemned all counterpopulation use of nuclear weapons and all first use of even the smallest counterforce nuclear weapons but did not categorically condemn the retaliatory use of all counterforce nuclear weapons. A motion was made from the floor and passed by the body of bishops to condemn all use of nuclear weapons. The logical conclusion of this resolution would be that the letter would then have to demand total unilateral nuclear disarmament. If you are not able to use any nuclear weapons, then you are not able to threaten to use any such weapons in a strategy of deterrence. Without totally developing the rationale Cardinal Bernardin later in the meeting strongly urged that the bishops retract the amendment they had earlier adopted which condemned all use of nuclear weapons. Ultimately the body of bishops did change their mind on this amendment, and thus the document did not condemn all use of nuclear weapons.[28] The reaction by Bernardin and others at this time indicates how significant was the judgment that there should be no call for total unilateral nuclear disarmament at the present time. Also strong indications surfaced from this discussion that not all the bishops realized how the rationale for this position was developed.

Without doubt the drafters of the pastoral struggled over the theory of deterrence, but from the very beginning through to the end they were clearly opposed to demanding unilateral nuclear disarmament at the present time. This judgment never wavered even though more theoretical considerations and principles were changed. The judgment about not demanding unilateral disarmament at the present time is a central part and even a cornerstone of the pastoral letter on peace and is not merely deduced from a more general principle. This comparatively long analysis has tried to prove that the pastoral letter on peace does not necessarily understand the judgment of conscience to be made in a deductive way by applying principles to particular cases.

Such a protracted analysis of the drafts of the pastoral letter on the economy will not be necessary to determine how it understands conscience to function. As already pointed out, the letter recognizes the different levels of moral principles and particular judgments and moves from principles to policies but does not explicitly describe the specific judgments as formed by applying principles to the particular historical circumstances. The principles interact with empirical data with historical, social, and political realities, and with competing demands on limited resources.[29]

The first draft of the pastoral letter on the economy structures itself by moving from the more general to the more specific. The first and most general consideration is a Christian vision of economic life, which for all practical purposes is a biblical vision. The next section proposes the ethical norms that should govern economic life and institutions. Part two involves policy applications, and in separate chapters treats the five specific issues of employment, poverty, food and agriculture, collaboration to shape the economy, and the United States and the world economy.[30] Archbishop Weakland, the chair of the committee drafting the economic pastoral, tried to respond to critics who found difficulty in what Weakland called the highly deductive nature of the first draft. As a result, the second draft avoids the strict division into the two parts of theory and application and also presents in a first chapter a descriptive focus on the signs of the times.[31] The final document follows the same basic approach but tries to avoid the deductive process of the first draft.

Conclusion

The conclusion of this analysis looks both to the past and to the future. In the recent past it seems that both the documents of the universal church social teaching and the recent pastoral letters of the United States bishops have attempted to safeguard the legitimate freedom of the conscience of the believer on specific, concrete social judgments and actions. Although the United States pastoral letters do make many prudential and specific judgments on policies and institutions, they recognize that others in the Christian community might disagree with them.

In their understanding of how conscience functions the older documents of the universal church teaching office often indicate that conscience works by applying universal principles to particular circumstances, by going from the general to the particular, and that by strict deduction. Later documents, especially as illustrated in *Octogesima Adveniens*, show that conscience decisions are not made by applying universal principles to particular circumstances or by moving rigorously from the more general to the more particular.

Many indications are present that the pastoral letter of the United States bishops on peace understands the decision of conscience to be made by the application of universal principles to particular circumstances. The document refers to the different levels of principles and the applications of principles. The content of the letter spells out the just-war criteria and then applies them. The letter definitely moves from the more general to the more specific. However, in reality it seems that a very significant judgment of conscience on not demanding unilateral nuclear disarmament at the present time was made by the bishops in a nondeductive manner. In fact, more general theoretical aspects and principles were even changed in the various drafts to make sure that this particular judgment could still logically be made. The second draft of the pastoral letter on the economy does overall move from the more general to the more specific but avoids speaking of specific judgments of conscience as the application of principles to changing circumstances and thus attempts to blunt the criticism that the first draft was too deductive. The final document follows the same approach. It seems to me that in following the directions from the January 1983 Vatican meeting to distinguish clearly between the level of universal principles and the level of application and by structuring their document by going from the more general to the more specific, the pastoral letters give the impression that judgments of conscience are formed deductively by moving from the abstract and the general to the concrete and the particular. However, as a matter of fact these documents do not see conscience as always or even often operating in this fashion.

Any future pastoral letter which makes such specific judgments and decisions on policies and actions should continue to safeguard the freedom of the believer. To safeguard this proper freedom pastoral letters must recognize that on more specific and complex matters a possible pluralism and diversity exist even within the church. Not only from the ecclesiological perspective but also from the perspective of systematic moral theology one should recognize different levels moving from the more general to the more specific. However, it should also be explicitly recognized that in the existential reality concrete judgments and decisions of a specific kind about the social order do not very often involve deduction or the movement from the abstract and general to the concrete and the particular. The United States bishops did not use deduction to arrive at their rejection of total unilateral nuclear disarmament. Discernment of conscience involving specific judgments is the most specific level of moral discourse and must logically be related to the more general levels, but such judgments are not necessarily made in the existential order by moving from the more general to the more specific. Logically such judgments must cohere with the more general understanding of perspectives, values, virtues, and principles, but such judgments in the existential order are formed in a more connatural and inductive way which does not follow deductive logic or a move from the abstract and general to the concrete and particular.

NOTES

1. Pastoral Constitution on the Church in the Modern World, par. 42,. in David J. O'Brien and Thomas A. Shannon, eds., *Renewing the Earth: Catholic Documents on Peace, Justice, and Liberation* (Garden City, NY: Doubleday Image Books, 1977), p. 216.

2. Pope Pius XI, *Quadragesimo Anno*, par. 11, in Terence P. McLaughlin, ed., *The Church and the Reconstruction of the Modern World: The Social Encyclicals of Pius XI* (Garden City, NY: Doubleday Image Books, 1957), p. 222.

3. Pope Pius XI, *Divini Redemptoris*, par. 34, in ibid., p. 379.

4. Pope John XXIII, *Mater et Magistra*, par. 226-242, in O'Brien and Shannon, *Renewing the Earth*, pp. 105-108.

5. Pope Paul VI, *Octogesima Adveniens*, par. 4, in ibid., pp. 353, 354.

6. Jean-Yves Calvez and Jacques Perrin, *The Church and Social Justice: The Social Teachings of the Popes from Leo XIII to Pius XII* (Chicago: Henry Regnery, 1961), pp. 58-62.

7. Marie-Dominque Chenu, *La "Doctrine Sociale" de L'Église Comme Ideologie* (Paris: Éditions du Cerf, 1979), especially pp. 79-96; Donal Dorr, *Options for the Poor: A Hundred Years of Vatican Social Teaching* (Maryknoll, NY: Orbis Books, 1983), pp. 157ff.

8. Benjamin L. Masse, *Justice for All: An Introduction to the Social Teaching of the Catholic Church* (Milwaukee: Bruce, 1964), pp. 70-88.

9. These different approaches are developed in my *American Catholic Social Ethics: Twentieth Century Approaches* (Notre Dame, IN: University of Notre Dame Press, 1982).

10. For a further development of this change see my *Directions in Catholic Social Ethics* (Notre Dame, IN: University of Notre Dame Press, 1985), pp. 5-42.

11. Pope John XXIII, *Mater et Magistra*, par. 236, in O'Brien and Shannon, *Renewing the Earth*, p. 107.

12. Pope John XXIII, *Mater et Magistra*, par. 217ff., in ibid., pp. 102ff.

13. Pope John XXIII, *Pacem in Terris*, par. 35-36, 80ff., in ibid., pp. 132, 142ff.

14. National Conference of Catholic Bishops, "The Challenge of Peace: God's Promise and Our Response," *Origins* 13 (1983): 1-32; National Conference of Catholic Bishops, "Economic Justice for All: Catholic Social Teaching and the U.S. Economy," *Origins* 16 (1986): 409-455.

15. "The Challenge of Peace," *Origins* 13 (1983): 3, 15.

16. J. Brian Benestad and Francis J. Butler, eds., *Quest for Justice: A Compendium of Statements of the United States Catholic Bishops on the Political and Social Order 1966-1980* (Washington, DC: National Conference of Catholic Bishops, 1981).

17. For a negative criticism of the bishops' approach see J. Brian Benestad, *The Pursuit of a Just Social Order: Policy Statements of the U.S. Catholic Bishops, 1966-1980* (Washington, DC: Ethics and Public Policy Center, 1982).

18. Archbishop Joseph Bernardin, "NCCB Committee Report: Studying War and Peace," *Origins* 11 (1981): 403, 404.

19. All this documentation is found in *Origins* 12 (1983): 690-696.

20. Ibid., p. 691.

21. Ibid., p. 693.

22. *Origins* 13 (1983): 2, 3.

23. *Origins* 16 (1986): nn. 134, 135; p. 426.

24. Ibid.

25. The first draft of the pastoral letter was not published in its entirety, but parts of it appeared in *National Catholic Reporter* 18 (July 2, 1982): 11ff. I am citing the document "First Draft: Pastoral Letter on Peace and War: God's Hope in a Time of Fear," which was sent to the bishops and others. The section on deterrence is found on pp. 25-38.

26. "Second Draft: Pastoral Letter on Peace and War," *Origins* 12 (1982): 315-318.

27. "Third Draft of Pastoral Letter: The Challenge of Peace: God's Promise and Our Response," *Origins* 12 (1983): 713-716. The teaching on deterrence in the final document is found in *Origins* 13 (1983): 16-19.

28. Jim Castelli, *The Bishops and the Bomb: Waging Peace in a Nuclear Age* (Garden City, NY: Doubleday Image Books, 1983), pp. 169, 170.

29. *Origins* 16 (1986): n. 134, p. 426.

30. "Pastoral Letter on Catholic Social Teaching and the U.S. Economy: First Draft," *Origins* 14 (1984): 337-383.

31. Rembert G. Weakland, "The Economic Pastoral: Draft Two," *America* (September 21, 1985): 129, 130.

10: Being Catholic and Being American

The story of Catholicism in the United States can best be understood in light of the struggle to be both Catholic and American. This question of being both Catholic and American is currently raised with great urgency in these days because of recent tensions between the Vatican and the Catholic Church in the United States.

History shows that the Vatican has always been suspicious and fearful that the American Catholic Church would become too American and in the process lose what is essential to its Roman Catholicism. Jay Dolan points out two historical periods in which attempts were made to incorporate more American approaches and understandings into the life of the church, but these attempts were ultimately unsuccessful.[1]

In the late eighteenth century the young Catholic Church in the United States attempted to appropriate many American ideas into its life. Recall that at this time the Catholic Church was a very small minority church. Dolan refers to this movement as a Republican Catholicism and links this understanding with the leading figure in the early American church, John Carroll. Carroll, before he was elected by the clergy as the first bishop in the United States in 1789, had asked Rome to grant to the church in the United States that ecclesiastical liberty which the temper of the age and of the people requires.

These early American Catholics wanted their church to reflect the spirit of the new nation. The early United States Catholic Church strongly supported religious toleration and

the separation of church and state. Carroll and most of the
clergy thought it was necessary to use English in the liturgy.
Democratization on the local level was attempted by the system of lay trustees who presided over the government of the
parish in temporal matters. However, this vision was soon
abandoned and never became a reality. A conservative mood
swept the entire country. John Carroll himself, after he became bishop, insisted more and more on authority and feared
the exercise of democracy and independence. Above all the
large influx of European clergy brought with them a different
understanding of Catholicism.

At the end of the nineteenth century another concentrated
move emerged for a more American Catholicism. A group
of bishops headed by Archbishop John Ireland of St. Paul,
with great support from Cardinal Gibbons, maintained that
the church must learn from the new age and from the American experience. However, in 1899 Pope Leo XIII condemned
Americanism. Cardinal Gibbons tried to soften the blow by
saying that no one in the United States ever held that "ex-
travagant and absurd doctrine."[2] There still remains some
doubt about the phantom heresy of Americanism,[3] but Leo
did condemn the desire to have "a church in America different
from that which is in the rest of the world." Catholicism does
not "admit modifications, according to the diversity of time
and place."[4]

The condemnation of Americanism was followed by the
condemnation of Modernism in 1907. This heresy according
to Pope Pius X corrupted the Catholic tradition and attempted
to apply scholarly and critical tools of analysis to scripture
studies and to theology. These condemnations were often cited
as the reason for the failure of the Roman Catholic Church
in the United States to develop any strong intellectual life.[5]
The defensive spirit behind these condemnations took hold
in the Catholic Church in the United States in the first half
of the twentieth century. American Catholicism heavily emphasized its distinctive Roman Catholic character.

Today the question of a more American Catholic Church
is being raised again in quite diverse circumstances. From
the psychological and sociological perspectives a great change

in Catholic self-identity in the United States has come about. Catholics are now in the mainstream of American life and society in terms of education, income, and leadership in many aspects of contemporary life. However, generalizations are somewhat difficult because the above statement is not true of most Catholic Hispanics. Since the Second Vatican Council the theological self-understanding has also changed quite dramatically. The pilgrim church emphasizes the people of God as distinguished from the older understanding of the church as a perfect society with primary emphasis given to its hierarchical structure. Above all Vatican Council II called for a dialogue with the modern world; no longer can the Catholic Church be seen as a ghetto structure defensively opposing all that is occurring in the modern world. Psychologically, sociologically, and theologically the Catholic Church in the United States after Vatican II is much more open to a dialogue with the American culture.

A United States Catholic in 1988 can too readily forget the tremendous changes that have occurred in Catholicism's own self-understanding and life in the last few decades. Philip Gleason described his feelings during the Catholic upheaval of the sixties as an impression of disintegration. He found the sixties devastating. "Indeed Catholics who had absorbed the mentality predominant in the generation before the Council had about the worst possible preparation for the sixties . . . overreaction to the excesses of the sixties, stands as a witness to the depth and extent of the changes which have occurred in the Roman Catholic Church in the United States in the last twenty-five years."[6]

Now the United States Catholic Church with its great theological, sociological, and psychological changes finds itself quite often in disagreement with the Vatican. The tensions between the Catholic Church in the United States and the Vatican have been growing for some time, but the differences are being felt more acutely at the present time. The Vatican has been investigating United States seminaries and United States religious women. Polls and pastoral experience show the gap between official Catholic moral teaching and the beliefs and actions of many Catholics in the area of sexuality.

Recall the action threatened by the Vatican against the religious women who signed a mildly pro abortion statement which was printed as an advertisement in *The New York Times.* In my case the Vatican has been willing to take a stand against me despite the fact that the vast majority of Catholic theologians in the United States have supported the legitimacy of my positions. The restrictions on Archbishop Hunthausen in Seattle created a very negative response not only in Seattle but throughout the Catholic Church in the United States. As a result of some American pressure the Vatican has restored full power to Archbishop Hunthausen. One prominent United States archbishop has publicly warned that these recent disciplinary actions by the Vatican against Roman Catholic leaders in the United States are alienating ordinary Catholics from the institutional church and could cause many to drift away from the life of the church.[7] Thus it is understandable that many people today are calling for a truly American Catholic Church.

Toward an American Catholic Church

Is it possible to have a truly American Catholic Church? From the viewpoint of the Catholic theological tradition one can find much support for the generic recognition of the church to be more American. This section will develop the reasons supporting the need for the church to become more American, whereas the next section will introduce some important cautions and corrections into the understanding of an American Catholic Church. The following seven reasons all support the generic position that the church can be a truly American Catholic Church. Many of these reasons were already mentioned in chapter three as the appealing aspects of Catholic theology and the generic justifications for the positions I have taken.

1) The Catholic tradition has consistently recognized that the word and work of Jesus must be made relevant and meaningful in the light of the historical and cultural circumstances of the day. Catholic theology has never accepted the famous

axiom "the scripture alone." Catholic theology has insisted on emphasizing the scripture and tradition. Yes, at times the axiom "the scripture and tradition" has been misunderstood. Both were thought of as two different and separate sources of revelation and truth. Also there has been the tendency to maintain that the tradition stopped fifty years before we were born. However, the proper understanding of tradition recognizes that the word and work of God must become present in the light of the changing circumstances of time and place.

History shows that the Catholic Church has recognized the need to make the word and work of Jesus meaningful and understood in the light of changing historical and cultural circumstances. In the fourth, fifth, and sixth centuries the church came to the understanding of the basic beliefs that there are three persons in God and two natures—the divine and the human—in the one person of Jesus. At that time some people objected that the church could not use such concepts or terminology because they were not found in the bible. The understanding of person and nature was borrowed from Greek philosophical thought and was not found in the scriptures. However, the early church found it necessary and helpful to use these contemporary thought patterns to understand better the very reality of God and Jesus.

The greatest theologian in the Roman Catholic Church is Thomas Aquinas (d. 1274). The genius of Aquinas was to use the contemporary thought patterns to understand and explain better the Christian mysteries. Aquinas was dissatisfied with just repeating what those before him had said. At that time Aristotelian thought had come into the university world of Europe. Aristotle never knew Jesus and probably did not believe in God, but Thomas Aquinas creatively incorporated Aristotelian thought into his theology. Thus the Catholic tradition has seen the need to make the word and work of Jesus understandable, meaningful, and present in the light of contemporary circumstances.

2) The Catholic tradition has taken the human and human reason very seriously. The Catholic insistence on "and" is seen not only in the emphasis on scripture and tradition but also in the acceptance of grace and nature, as well as faith and

reason. The Catholic tradition has always given a great importance to the human even apart from grace. Both the supernatural and the natural are important. According to a famous axiom of Catholic theology and spirituality, grace does not destroy nature but grace builds on nature. At times this approach did not adequately put together grace and nature, but it has always recognized the basic goodness and importance of the human. The glory of God according to an often-quoted statement of the early church is the human person come alive. Catholic theology has seen God as working in and through secondary human causes.

In addition to its emphasis on grace and nature, and grace and the human, the Catholic tradition has also accepted the importance of faith and reason. Medieval Scholastics boldly asserted that faith and reason can never contradict one another. This is a magnificent statement of faith in the goodness of human reason itself. The medieval church saw the quest for knowledge and the establishment of universities as an important part of its own mission.

The insistence on the basic goodness of the human and human reason is exemplified especially in Catholic moral theology with its natural-law methodology. From the theological perspective natural law has been the answer to a fundamental methodological question—Where does the Christian find ethical wisdom and knowledge? Is this wisdom found only in Jesus and in revelation? The Catholic response was that wisdom is also found in human nature and human reason. The natural law is best understood in the Thomistic tradition as human reason directing human beings to their end in accord with their nature. Catholic moral theology has relied very heavily on the natural-law methodology for its moral teachings. Today there are many criticisms of natural law, especially from the philosophical perspective with regard to the meaning of reason and the meaning of nature. However, Catholic moral theology continues to rely heavily on the human and human reason.

3) Catholic ecclesiology has insisted on the incarnational principle. The incarnation means that Jesus became truly human at a particular time and place in human history. Cath-

olic theology has given great importance to the recognition
that all that is human has been touched by and brought into
the mystery of the divine. Catholic sacramentology sees visible human signs involving the basic human realities of cele-
brating, eating, drinking, and anointing as ways through
which the divine is mediated to us. Catholic ecclesiology insists on a visible church — not merely an invisible church.
Human persons and human institutions are mediators of the
divine presence and gift. The church is divine and human.
No other Christian ecclesiology gives as much importance to
the human aspect and the visible structure of the church. The
church like Jesus must become incarnate in time and space.
The Catholic Church gives a strong emphasis to the human
element even though at times the human element will get in
the way of, rather than mediate, the divine reality.

4) History reminds us that the church has adapted itself
to the prevailing historical and cultural human realities. The
Catholic Church today would look quite different if it had
not taken root in the soil of Rome during its beginnings. The
church borrows much from the Roman way of administration and acting. To this day church laws heavily depend upon
Roman law and not upon the common law that is the basis
of the Anglo-Saxon legal system. Recall that until a few years
ago Latin was even the official liturgical language of the entire church.

A knowledge of history also serves to overcome the "ahistorical orthodoxy" that identifies authentic Catholicity with
a period just before the Second Vatican Council. There can
be no doubt that this period marked the apex of an overly
authoritarian understanding of the church. Ever since the sixteenth century the Roman Catholic Church assumed a defensive attitude against the Protestant Reformation and against
the modern world. In this defensive position the church insisted that it alone had truth. The Catholic Church opposed
the philosophical, scientific, and political aspects of modernity. The Syllabus of Errors in the nineteenth century and
the later condemnations of Americanism and Modernism all
testified to this very defensive and authoritarian understanding of the church and its structures. At the same time the

growing technology of modern transportation and of communication helped to promote the overly centralized, authoritarian understanding and structure of the Roman Catholic
Church. As a result of these developments the Vatican could
be in immediate contact with the entire world and thus exercise its authority much more readily and easily.

Vatican Council II in the early 1960s introduced a sweep-
ing change in Catholicism. The emphasis was on the need
to respect the autonomy of human culture and institutions
and to dialogue with the modern world. Thus the Catholic
Church instituted its dialogue with modernity which had been
artificially delayed for almost four centuries. At the same time
the church opened the door to ecumenism and the need to
dialogue with other Christians, Jews, and all religious and
even nonreligious peoples. The Vatican Council also renewed
the church's own self-understanding. The metaphors most
frequently used to understand the church were the people of
God and the pilgrim church. The church was not changing
its hierarchical structure, but this was seen in the service of
the pilgrim people of God.

Without doubt the changes of the Second Vatican Council were deep and far reaching, but they were in keeping with
the best of the Catholic tradition with its recognition of the
need to make the word and work of Jesus meaningful within
changing historical and cultural circumstances. This call for
dialogue with the modern world reflected the Catholic tradition's insistence on the goodness of the human and of human
reason.

History expands our horizons by pointing out that things
have not always been the same in the Catholic Church's self-
understanding or institutional structure. The Vatican II renewal of the church was also rooted in a knowledge that in
history the church had taken on different understandings and
forms. The Catholic Church insists on the importance of the
role of pope and bishops in the church, but history reminds
us of the different ways these offices have functioned and been
related to one another. Recall that even in the early United
States Father Carroll and the first leaders of the church wanted
the bishops elected by the local clergy. Thus history teaches

us the diversity that has existed within Roman Catholicism and the possibility of other changes today.

5) The history of American Catholicism reminds us that the Catholic Church has adapted to and learned from the United States cultural ethos and political system.[8] The primary question often raised in the past was whether Catholicism could fully accept the United States political self-understanding with its emphasis on freedom, religious freedom, and the separation of church and state. History reminds us of the tensions that brought about a dramatic change in Catholic self-understanding in this country.

In the nineteenth century the Catholic Church was opposed to freedom and rejected the United States political system of religious freedom. In the twentieth century Roman Catholicism began to face a different enemy or dialogue partner—totalitarian governments and movements. In this context Catholic teaching began to defend the freedom and dignity of the individual person against the encroachments of totalitarian government. Catholic social teaching traditionally claimed that it was open to all forms of political government, but little by little its support for democracy began to develop. As we have seen before, the first detailed development of human rights in official Catholic social teaching appeared only in Pope John XXIII's encyclical *Pacem in Terris* in 1963.[9] Before that time Catholic teaching stressed duties and not rights, because the concept of rights seemed to favor a one-sided individualism.

As noted in chapter five, the growing Catholic acceptance of freedom, rights, and human dignity on the universal level was in tension with the older teaching affirming the union of church and state and denying religious freedom. In the 1950s John Courtney Murray in the United States, Jacques Maritain in France, and others stressed the need for the church to accept religious freedom. Finally at Vatican II the church teaching changed with the recognition that the fathers of Vatican II had learned from history and the experience of Christian people the importance of religious freedom.[10] Without doubt the church did learn from the experience of Catholicism in the United States. This change was arduous, slow, and not without considerable pain, but the Roman Catholic Church finally came to accept the American understanding of religious freedom.

6) Catholic teaching has recently recognized that the church, which calls for justice in the world and in civil society, must be just itself. The 1971 Synod of Bishops declared: "While the church is bound to give witness to justice, she recognizes that everyone who ventures to speak to people about justice must first be just in their eyes. Hence we must undertake an examination of the modes of acting and of the possessions and lifestyle found within the church herself."[11] The document then stresses the different rights which must be present even in the church — the right to a living wage, the right of lay people to share in the administration of church property, the right of women to participate in the life of the church, the right to suitable freedom and expression of thought, the right to just procedures in court cases, the right to know one's accusers, the right to have some share in decision-making in the church.

In the same year of 1971 Pope Paul VI in his apostolic letter *Octogesima Adveniens* underlied two important aspirations that become more and more prevalent in the contemporary context, and they grow stronger to the extent that human beings become better informed and better educated: "the aspiration to equality and the aspiration to participation — two forms of human dignity and freedom."[12] Without denying its basic structure, the church recognizes the need to promote justice, rights, and a greater participation by all, especially women, in the life of the church.

7) Contemporary church teaching has recognized the importance of historical consciousness and its consequences. The primary change in Catholic self-understanding at the Second Vatican Council was the recognition of historical consciousness. Bernard Lonergan and other have contrasted historical consciousness with classicism.[13] Classicism stresses the eternal, the immutable, and unchanging. The danger of classicism is to identify the eternal plan of God with what is in reality a historically relative condition. Classicism generally employs a deductive methodology; historical consciousness gives greater

imporance to the individual and the historical and uses a more inductive methodology.

The general comparison made in chapter five between the 1931 encyclical *Quadragesimo Anno* of Pope Pius XI and the 1971 letter *Octogesima Adveniens* of Pope Paul VI well illustrates the difference between a classicist and a historically conscious approach. Pope Pius XI's encyclical is entitled in English "On Reconstructing the Social Order," which attempts to develop a blueprint that should be put into practice throughout the world.[14] Using an approach best described as a moderate corporatism or solidarism, the pope maintains that the different parties in the social and economic order — owners, workers, and consumers — should work together to determine what happens in a particular industry. Then there would be higher levels of such cooperation, dealing with the relationship among the various industries. At the time of Pope John XXIII in the 1960s official Catholic teaching stopped talking about this plan for reconstruction, a plan that was deduced in the abstract and never really had a chance of being applied in the concrete contemporary historical situations.

In 1971 Pope Paul VI took a very different approach from his predecessor forty years earlier. "In the face of such widely varying situations, it is difficult for us to utter a unified message and to put forward a solution which has universal validity. Such is not our ambition, nor is it our mission. It is up to the Christian communities to analyze with objectivity the situation which is proper to their own country, to shed on it the light of the gospel's unalterable words, and to draw principles of reflection, norms of judgment, and directives for action from the social teaching of the church."[15] Here is an explicit recognition of local diversity because of different situations and circumstances.

Some recognition of local diversity in ecclesiology is evidenced with the acceptance of the structures of regional and national conferences of bishops. In the United States and elsewhere (e.g., South America) a much greater involvement of regional and national conferences of bishops in dealing with local problems exists.

Thus all these considerations indicate the legitimacy of and

the need for the Amercian Catholic Church to be in dialogue
with its own culture and to incorporate many aspects of that
culture in its own self-understanding and structure.

Clarifications and Cautions

Legitimate and necessary it is to talk about the American
Catholic Church which can and should incorporate into its
self-understanding, its life, and its structures what is best in
the American ethos and culture. However, important clarifica-
tions and cautions must be made. The first caution is a linguistic one. Our language needs an adjective to correspond
with United States. We are not the only Americans in the
world; we are not even the only North Americans in the
world. To speak about the American Catholic Church is in-
correct if we are referring only to the church in the United
States. However, at the present time our linguistic poverty
means no adjective exists to describe properly and specifically
the United States.

A second caution concerns the danger of making overgen-
eralizations about the United States ethos and culture. A great
deal of diversity abounds regarding the United States in general and United States Catholicism specifically. One can point
to certain characteristics that predominate within the United
States culture in general and Catholic self-understanding in
particular, but one must always be aware of the danger of
overgeneralization in the midst of so much pluralism and
diversity in the United States.

A third danger is the fact that some people in the United
States tend to see the whole problem too narrowly. Many
Catholics in the United States are very conscious of the tensions between the Vatican and the Roman Catholic Church
in the United States, but they forget about the tensions between the Vatican and many other parts of the world. The
basic question we are dealing with is the unity of the church
and its diversity on different local levels. How can the church
be one and at the same time allow for legitimate differences
because of local conditions and culture? In the 1960s a recog-

nition in theory of the need for such unity and diversity was growing, but the problem now is to work this out institutionally and in practice.

An analogy from Catholic social teaching might help. Catholic social teaching has always tried to avoid the two opposite dangers of collectivism and individualism. In a true society or community one must protect the rights of the individuals while still maintaining the fabric of community and society in the working together of all for the common good. The principle of subsidiarity has been used in Catholic thought to govern the respective roles of all concerned in society.[16] According to this principle the larger groups exist as a help to the individual and smaller associations or institutions within society. Individuals and smaller groupings should be enabled and empowered to do all they can. The larger associations and institutions, including the state, should be involved only in those things which the smaller associations and individuals cannot do alone. There is no reason why the principle of subsidiarity cannot be applied in an analogous way to the life of the church. However, the issues must be seen in their totality, which is much more than merely the problem of the Vatican and the United States.

A fourth caution stresses the transcendence of the word of God. Yes, the church must be in dialogue with contemporary society, but a part of that dialogue involves a negative criticism of what is happening in all contemporary society. The church at times must learn from human culture, but at times it must criticize and correct it. Human limitation and sinfulness will affect all human culture and activity. The earlier section pointed out how the church has learned from the emphasis in the United States on freedom, human rights, and the need for participation by all. However, some characteristics of the United States ethos and culture need to be criticized in the light of the gospel. The gospel itself transcends every culture and serves as a negative critique of all existing human realities.

Recent history reminds us that there was a tendency in the United States for Catholics not to be critical enough of the American ethos, culture, and political system. In certain aspects the Catholic Church in the United States became too American and lost its critical perspective. In the 1960s the identification between being Catholic and being American seemed to reach its apex. The election of a Catholic president indicated that other Americans were no longer suspicious of Catholics as being inferior citizens. Catholics had recently entered into the mainstream of American life and culture from the sociological and economic perspectives. The acceptance of religious freedom at Vatican II seemed to put the final seal of approval on the fact one could be Catholic and American at the same time. However, in the 1960s the problems of racism, poverty, and militarism raised their ugly heads. Instead of stressing the basic compatibility between being Catholic and being American some Catholics now stressed the need for Catholicism to be a negative critique of the existing American culture. Thus recent American Catholic history reminds us of the danger of losing the critical element which must always be associated with the gospel and the church.

In the recent pastoral letters on peace and the economy the United States bishops have engaged in a true dialogue with United States culture and self-understanding and at times have put forth negative criticisms of what is happening in the United States ethos. A superpower always faces the temptation to use power excessively and for the wrong reasons and not to respect the freedom and rights of other less powerful nations and persons. The pastoral letter on the economy rightly points out the great danger of individualism in the American culture with its repercussions for all aspects of the economic order. More emphasis must be given to social justice and to the recognition that the goods of creation exist to serve the needs of all people. In addition, the materialism and consumerism in the United States deserve to be heavily criticized. Yes, there must be a dialogue between the church and contemporary culture. At times the church will learn from the culture, but at times it must negatively criticize the culture and stand up to it.

A fifth caution concerns the fundamental differences between the church and any political society. However, it must be pointed out that Catholic theology with its emphasis on visible structures has always been more open to see an analogy between the church and other political societies. The church and faith have an authoritative character about them and transcend reason and all secular institutions, but at the same time this church institution must become incarnate. One can and should call for greater freedom, justice, and participation of all in existing church structures without in any way denying the divine aspect of the church.

A final caution or correction comes from the need to distinguish more clearly two aspects of the problem. The first aspect is the more general one pertaining to the universal church, which involves the need for creative fidelity to the word and work of Jesus. This creative fidelity means that what has been handed down from apostolic times must be made meaningful and appropriated in the contemporary historical and cultural circumstances. Many of the issues that are often discussed in the context of American Catholicism (e.g., a greater participation by all in the life of the church, the need for more just structures to protect individual rights) really pertain to the whole church and not only to the church in the United States. Some tension will always be evident in the church between past and present precisely because the church community is involved with a living tradition.

The second aspect is the tension between universality and particularity. This is the case in which one would most appropriately speak of those things that are peculiar to the United States situation and not to others. For example, one can think of the need to recognize the Hispanic traditions which are now so important a part of the life of the church in the United States. To sort out in practice these two different aspects of the question will very often be difficult, but to recognize the two different sources of tension is important.

Conclusions about the Present and the Future

Thus in a proper sense one can speak of the American Catholic Church, but with all the nuances and cautions mentioned in the last section. The church will always experience the twofold tension that arises from the need for the church to be creatively faithful to the word and work of Jesus and from the recognition that the church must preserve both universality and particularity. All of us must exhibit the love, respect, and patience which are necessary for a community to retain its own identity in the midst of these tensions. The call to all in the church is to make sure that these tensions are creative and serve the life of the church.

At the present time, however, these tensions are greatly heightened for three different reasons. As a result the contemporary Catholic Church in the United States is going to experience even more problems in the immediate future.

The first reason for greatly heightened strains comes from the theoretical view of the Catholic Church with its inevitable tensions between fidelity and creativity and between universality and particularity. As described in the last few pages I maintain this understanding is rooted in the best of the Catholic tradition and has been reasserted again by the Second Vatican Council. However, some in the church today do not share this view.

Much of the unnecessary tension between theologians in the church and the Vatican hierarchical teaching office at the present time comes from the fact that the Vatican still tends to think of Catholic theology only in the terms of ahistorical neo-Scholasticism. As a result increasing frictions have surfaced between Roman authorities and theologians throughout the world who have rightly been employing different types of methodological approaches. At the same time some Roman officials are trying to downplay the doctrinal significance and practical role of regional and national conferences of bishops.[17] Thus a theoretical reluctance remains on the part of some to accept a legitimate role for creativity and particularity.

The second reason for the exaggerated tensions at the present time is a structural one. The United States Catholic bishops in their two recent pastoral letters on peace and the economy have recognized that social change involves both a change of heart and a change of structures. Unfortunately at the present time those structures which should embody the understanding of the church proposed above are very weak and insufficient.

The Second Vatican Council gave greater importance to the collegiality of all the bishops of the church and recognized the need for regional and national conferences of bishops. The Synod of Bishops was established as a vehicle to make collegiality a living reality in the life of the church. On more local levels a growing importance has been given to the involvement and participation of all in the life of the church through parish and diocesan councils, councils of priests and assemblies of women religious and other similar groups. Yes, some significant changes have been attempted to embody the newer understandings of the church, but more and better structures are urgently needed.

In the context of the present tensions being experienced in the United States Catholic Church the bridge between the United States Church and the Vatican is for all practical purposes basically the United States bishops. However, the regional and national conferences of bishops, the Synod of Bishops, and the whole structure of collegiality are woefully inadequate at the present time. The Roman Catholic Church is still highly centralized in Rome. Bishops' conferences have very little power. The Synods of Bishops, which have been held periodically, have not really been free and honest discussions of problems facing the church. These meetings have been heavily controlled by Roman officials. As a result, no really adequate structure exists to make truly present the two-way dialogue between Rome and the particular churches.

The collegiality of bishops will never be a reality until individual bishops or a group of bishops can publicly express disagreement with the pope on certain issues, even those belonging to the noninfallible church teaching on faith and morals. Yes, the pope has the Petrine office in the church and is the head of the church as well as its symbol of unity, but the pope can be wrong. Bishops must be in a position within this community of bishops to freely and forthrightly state their opinions. At the present time we really do not have viable structures to make collegiality a living reality in the life of the church.

A third reason why heightened and exaggerated tensions will continue to exist in the American Catholic Church in the immediate future is that the issues and problems causing the stress are not going to go away. In fact the questions and issues will become even more intense. One does not have to be a sociologist or a prophet to know that the major issue facing the Catholic Church in the United States in the next few years will be the role of women in the church. This question directly touches a great number of people who form a large critical mass which will make this issue be felt throughout the church. At the present time many Catholic women are becoming more and more disenchanted with the church. Catholic teaching in social ethics has recognized the need for greater equality and participation of women in all aspects of human existence. Many of us perceive that the same aspirations to equality and participation must be made much more present in the life of the church. Women are now assuming more roles in the church than they did in the past, but it would not be unfair to dismiss what is happening at the present time as mostly tokenism.

The issue of the participation of women in ordained ministry and in the total life of the church is a structural issue and cannot be solved without a dramatic change of structures. Other issues can be solved much more easily without having to change structures. For example, in conscience many married United States Catholics have decided to practice artificial contraception. They have made this decision in good conscience and continue to participate in the life of the church. Likewise, some divorced and remarried Catholics continue to participate fully in the Eucharist. In such cases no need exists for structural change. However, no greater participation of women in the ministry and the life of the church can come about without great structural change.

In the near future the tensions existing in the Roman Catholic Church in the United States will continue to grow. However, in the long run I am convinced that the Catholic tradition is open to the changes that are necessary. The Catholic tradition itself firmly supports the need for creative fidelity concerning the word and work of Jesus and also justifies the importance of a greater voice for the local churches. At the same time the Catholic tradition has always recognized the importance of structures and institutions in the Church. The process of continual reform in the Roman Catholic Church thus calls for an ongoing education on the one hand and the need for new structures on the other. The need for creative fidelity and the role of local and national churches must continue to be emphasized. The existing fragile structures which give more importance to collegiality and the participation of all in the life of the church must be greatly strengthened and increased.

There is a legitimate sense in which one can and must speak about a church which is both Roman Catholic and American. There should always be a tension which hopefully is creative between past and present in the church and between the universal and the particular churches. The tension between Rome and the American Church at the present time seems to be more negative than creative, and these negative aspects will probably grow stronger in the short-term future. I am convinced that in the long term the Catholic Church has the theory to deal with these tensions creatively, but we urgently need both proper education and appropriate structures to overcome the strident, destructive, and negative aspects of these tensions currently experienced.

NOTES

1. Jay P. Dolan, "American Catholicism and Modernity," *Cross Currents* 31 (1981-82): 150-162. See also Jay P. Dolan, *The American Catholic Experience* (Garden City, NY: Doubleday, 1985).

2. For the text of Cardinal Gibbons' letter to the pope see Thomas T. McAvoy, *The Great Crisis in American Catholic History 1895-1900* (Chicago: Henry Regnery, 1957), p. 286.

3. Margaret M. Reher, "Leo XIII and 'Americanism'," *Theological Studies* 34 (1973): 679-689.

4. Leo XIII, *Testem Benevolentiae*, in McAvoy, *The Great Crisis in American Catholic History*, pp. 379-391. The citations in the text are found on pp. 381-382 and 390.

5. Michael V. Gannon, "Before and After Modernism: The Intellectual Isolation of the American Priest," in John Tracy Ellis, ed., *The Catholic Priest in the United States: Historical Investigations* (Collegeville, MN: St. John's University Press, 1971), pp. 293-383.

6. Philip Gleason, "In Search of Unity: American Catholic Thought, 1920-1960," *The Catholic Historical Review* 65 (1979): 189.

7. *New York Times*, October 9, 1986, p. 10.

8. For recent histories of American Catholicism see Jay P. Dolan, *The American Catholic Experience* (Garden City, NY: Doubleday, 1985); Gerald P. Fogarty, *The Vatican and the American Hierarchy from 1870 to 1965* (Wilmington, DE: Michael Glazier, 1985); James J. Hennessey, *American Catholics: A History of the Roman Catholic Community in the United States* (New York: Oxford University Press, 1981).

9. Pope John XXIII, *Pacem in Terris*, nn. 11-27, in David J. O'Brien and Thomas A. Shannon, eds., *Renewing the Earth: Catholic Documents on Peace, Justice, and Liberation* (Garden City, NY: Doubleday Image Books, 1977), pp. 126-130.

10. Richard J. Regan, *Conflict and Consensus: Religious Freedom and the Second Vatican Council* (New York: Macmillan, 1967).

11. Synod of Bishops, *Justitia in Mundo*, in O'Brien and Shannon, *Renewing the Earth*, p. 400.

12. Pope Paul VI, *Octogesima Adveniens*, n. 22, in ibid., p. 364.

13. Bernard Lonergan, *Method in Theology* (New York: Herder and Herder, 1972), pp. 181ff.

14. Pope Pius XI, *Quadragesimo Anno* ("On Reconstructing the Social Order") in Terence P. McLaughlin, ed., *The Church and the Reconstruction of the Modern World: The Social Encyclicals of Pius XI* (Garden City, NY: Doubleday Image Books, 1957), pp. 219-278.

15. Pope Paul VI, *Octogesima Adveniens*, n. 4, in O'Brien and Shannon, *Renewing the Earth*, pp. 353, 354.

16. Pope Pius XI, *Quadragesimo Anno*, nn. 79, 80, in McLaughlin, *The Church and the Reconstruction of the Modern World*, pp. 246, 247; Pope John XXIII, *Mater et Magistra*, nn. 51-58, in O'Brien and Shannon, *Renewing the Earth*, pp. 62-64.

17. Joseph Cardinal Ratzinger with Vittorio Messori, *The Ratzinger Report* (San Francisco, CA: Ignatius Press, 1985), pp. 58-61.

Index

3,74,75,76